CURIOSITIES SERIES

Connecticut
CURIOSITIES

QUIRKY CHARACTERS, ROADSIDE ODDITIES & OTHER OFFBEAT STUFF

SUSAN CAMPBELL
AND
BILL HEALD

SECOND EDITION

INSIDERS' GUIDE®

GUILFORD, CONNECTICUT
AN IMPRINT OF THE GLOBE PEQUOT PRESS

INSIDERS' GUIDE ®

Cover and interior photos by the authors
Text design by Nancy Freeborn
Layout by Debbie Nicolais
Maps by Rusty Nelson © Morris Book Publishing, LLC

ISBN–13: 978-0-7627-4103-8
ISBN–10: 0-7627-4103-1

Manufactured in the United States of America
Second Edition/First Printing

To all Connecticut residents—
past, present, and future.

CONNECTICUT

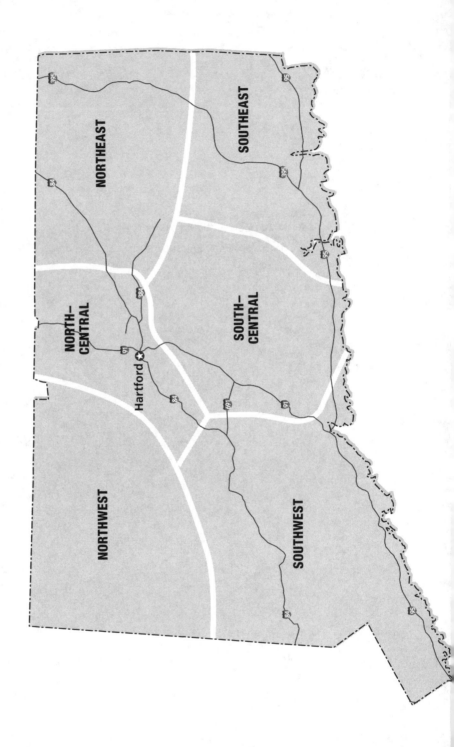

Contents

Acknowledgments

We wish to thank Danielle Rigby, Frank Schiavone, Samuel Bruder, Ryan Schiavone, Tina Jeter (who still rides great shotgun), Colin McEnroe, and the countless curious contributors to this volume who took time out to talk to us.

Introduction

At first glance, Connecticut might not look too special compared with a lot of other states. It's basically a big rectangle, unlike geographically shapely states like Florida or Italy. Granted, Italy isn't a state, but it's certainly more interesting to look at on a map than a place resembling a big credit card with a tail.

We Nutmeggers are also saddled with a lack of major league sports franchises. We have no enormous movie studios (yet), no Silicon Valley, and no signature dish (like Texas has chili or California has tofu). New Jersey has Bruce Springsteen, Alaska has Jewel, and Oklahoma has Merle Haggard. Even Hawaii has Don Ho—and they're way out in the middle of the ocean, for crying out loud.

Given this apparent lack of "color," when we were asked to write a book about the crazy, wacky side of Connecticut we were initially skeptical. "Where is the wackiness?" we asked. "Our Connecticut neighbors are pragmatic, sensible New England types. Where's the beef, in terms of outlandish antics?"

Come to find out, the wackiness is around the next corner, in Willimantic, in the form of giant frogs. The beef is found in a beat-up diner that sells gourmet food. Connecticut displays its off-the-wall uniqueness in the creative power that turns a backyard garage into the source of silky horsepower for some of the world's most exotic cars (like Aston-Martins) or the innovative thinking that produced, quite possibly, the nation's first pizza.

In these pages you will discover, as we did, that Connecticut harbors strange, unusual, and wonderfully funny people who do some pretty bizarre and fascinating things. Did we uncover wackiness? You bet, but more often than not it is a subtle wackiness that manifests itself in sophisticated ways. Connecticut residents have created submarines—and chronicled political events in ostrich eggs. The first penny was minted inside our borders, and we have the oldest continuously published daily newspaper. We have an incredible history here, and the more you poke around, the wilder it gets.

Poking around, by the way, is the only way to truly see the more unusual treasures that Connecticut has to offer. This is a small-town, nook-and-cranny type of state—a well-populated yet highly private territory where you can easily miss a dinosaur parked in the backyard of a typical suburban dwelling if you're not keeping a wary eye out. Even our geology is interesting, for if a rock isn't engaging enough on its own, someone will paint the sucker so that it literally stops traffic.

We mentioned history, and Connecticut has more than its share. As one of the original thirteen colonies, our revolutionary heritage is found all over the place, and our legends are, well, legend. And in terms of historic hardware, there are many old yet incredibly well-preserved artifacts in this state.

Among notable Connecticut births, the Wiffle ball reigns supreme.

Some of these relics are rather unusual; we tend to cherish some items that less-enlightened individuals might throw away. Fire a cannonball into one of our taverns during a Revolutionary War battle, and we're likely to keep the ordnance for hundreds of years as an alternative home decoration. Our weathervanes last for centuries, even after inebriated soldiers pepper them with bullets. When our Colonial farmers built walls, they lasted to the present day, even though the builders used no mortar of any type.

Ours is a state where Mark Twain once roamed and where he passed his last days on earth. His particular brand of honesty, integrity, humor, and invention fit Connecticut like his trademark white suit. Wiffle balls—those weird, perforated plastic baseballs that have spared many an urban window from destruction—began life in Connecticut. We have tall, brawny flagpoles and extremely short ferries. Our gardens are unique, our cuisine is remarkable, our oaks are patriotic. We still hand-bottle soda pop and have a parade for boomboxes that will never rival Macy's affair but has a homespun-genuinely-weird quality that dwarfs the aura of even the mightiest helium-filled balloon.

Intrigued? So were we as we traveled around exploring Connecticut's hidden crazier attractions. We now invite you to join us in these pages and explore the singular wonders that make Connecticut unique, entertaining—and even, yes, wacky. A big rectangle? Hah! That rectangle is a canvas depicting a wild, colorful world painted by some of the most talented and quirky artists on the planet. Enjoy!

NORTHWEST

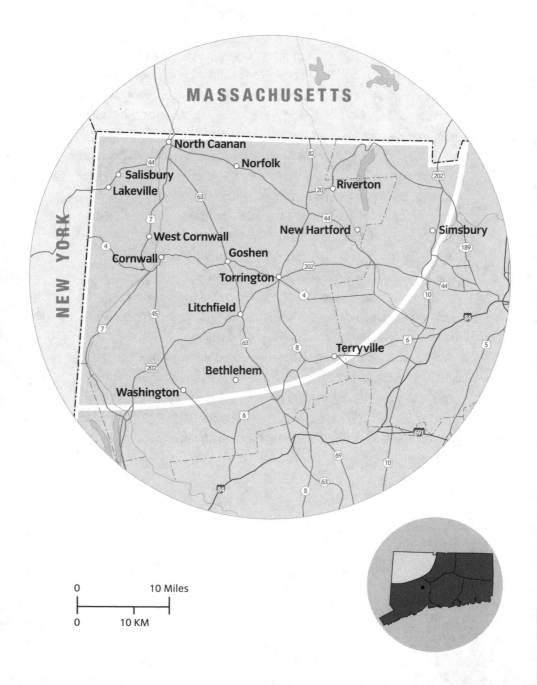

MASSACHUSETTS

NEW YORK

North Caanan
Norfolk
Salisbury
Lakeville
Riverton
West Cornwall
New Hartford
Simsbury
Cornwall
Goshen
Torrington
Litchfield
Terryville
Bethlehem
Washington

0   10 Miles

0   10 KM

NORTHWEST

Kicking the Hollywood Habit

Bethlehem

In the late 1950s, Dolores Hart was a Hollywood starlet with a bullet.
She was a Princess Grace look-alike with a natural screen presence—so
natural that her first screen appearance was with Elvis Presley in *Loving
You.* In the next six short years, she appeared in ten other films, including another Presley film, *King Creole,* and the classic teen-angst flick
Where the Boys Are. In that one she was the carefree girl who dove
fully clothed into a club's huge fish tank.

Life was good, but Dolores had visited the Abbey of Regina Laudis in
Bethlehem on retreat, and she kept finding herself back at the abbey's
wooden gate. In 1963 a studio limo once more dropped off Dolores,
then twenty-four, with the Benedictines and their Gregorian chant, and
after two weeks she knew she would stay. She briefly returned to her
worldly life to say good-bye. She told her stunned but supportive
fiancé, her incredulous family, and producer Hal Wallis, who could not
believe she'd throw away her future for a cloistered life. She has lived
the simple life of a nun since.

Mother Dolores, sixty-eight, is not the only Regina Laudis nun to have
turned her back on a successful secular life. There are lawyers and politi-
cians—even a member of royalty—and each nun stays as connected to

her past life and profession as her order allows. Mother Dolores is still a member of the Academy of Motion Picture Arts and Sciences and gets videos of first-run movies. By the way, she loved *Dead Man Walking* and was stunned at the rawness of *Saving Private Ryan*.

IF THE SHOE FITS. . .

The Nutmeg State recently earned a new nickname in publications around the country: Corrupticut. Seems our elected officials had a run of bad judgment. Our former governor resigned and went to jail on a corruption-related charge. Several of his minions did as well. Two of our mayors, in rather short order, went to jail—one for corruption, and one for particularly heinous sex offenses involving preteen girls. We are so very sorry. We've always liked to make fun of, say, New Jersey or Rhode Island for this kind of nonsense, but no less an authority than the *New York Times* called us "Corrupticut," so it must be true.

Where Things Go Bump around the Clock

Cornwall

Near the thriving city of Cornwall is a group of foundation remnants and cellar holes that once was the village of Dudleytown—also known as Village of the Damned.

If that doesn't get your ghostbuster blood flowing, you need to check your pulse.

Legend is that a nineteenth-century curse led to the desertion of this town, located off a little-used path now known as Dark Entry Road. For some reason early settlers ignored that the land was too rocky for cultivation and the area too far removed from a ready water source. Add to those problems the dimness of Dudleytown, which is constantly in the shadows of the surrounding hills.

The legend varies, but boiled down, the town was abandoned after an uncomfortably large number of town residents went insane or succumbed to sudden, violent deaths. One researcher says that the town may have suffered from a kind of collective madness that could be traced to its forebears in England. Some say the early families of the town's inhabitants once tried to usurp the English crown and for their troubles were beheaded and cursed. Others say that since the rocks in the area are lousy with lead, the groundwater must be also. The only thing we know for sure is that by 1899 no one lived in Dudleytown, and the forest moved back in.

These days—other than the holes in the ground—all that remains are reported orbs of light that swirl around in the gloom. Hikers swear that birds and forest animals do not enter the boundaries of the hamlet, and, sure enough, the woods thereabouts are eerily silent. Or maybe that's just our imagination. Dudleytown is just south of Coltsfoot Mountain. Take Route 7 south from Cornwall Bridge. About 2 miles down the road you'll find Dark Entry Road on the left. Enter at your own risk. The owners don't want visitors.

CUE THE CAMEL!

Where do movie producers go when they need an exotic animal—and they need it for a film shoot in Connecticut? The Connecticut Film Commission has a list of companies that provide said beasts, but one of the first ones producers think of is R.W. Commerford & Sons, of Goshen. Commerford & Sons are able to locate and transport some of the most amazing animals—including, of course, the aforementioned humped beastie.

The company also specializes in petting zoos and animal exhibits that include miniature horses, a camel, and a 4,000-pound elephant. It supplies reindeer for Christmas parties and other animals for the advertising campaigns of companies as diverse as Brooks Brothers and Toys 'R' Us. And without it, Hartford's Three Kings Day parades would be without their much-loved camels.

R.W. Commerford & Sons, Inc., is at 48 Torrington Road (Route 4). Call (860) 491–3421 for more information, or visit their Web site at www.commerfordzoo.com.

They'll Smoke 'Em If You've Got 'Em

Goshen

Sure, anyone can get you a smoked ham or turkey, but how about smoked pheasant, shrimp, and venison? And what to do with that large roadkill? Can't let that go to waste, can you?

OK, we're kidding about the roadkill, but for two generations Nodine's Smokehouse has been turning out specialized fare for the learned palate.

Nonsmokers can try the wild boar, buffalo, and quail. On our visit to the Goshen store, we found buffalo burgers and buffalo steaks alongside hot and sweet Italian sausages.

But do you know what we really liked? The store offers Yankee link sausage, English-style bangers, crawfish boudin, and alligator.

Smokehouse tours are available if you call in advance. Free tastings are held every Columbus Day weekend. Nodine's Smokehouse plant is in Torrington, and the retail store is in Goshen on Route 63, just 1,000 yards north of where it intersects with Route 4. Call (800) 222–2059 or (860) 491–4009, or visit nodinesmokehouse .com for more information.

Here's the view outside Nodine's retail shop.

The Child as Wandering Rodent
Lakeville

You love them more than anything, but there are times you want to keep them occupied so that you can have some time to yourself. Obviously we're referring to children and not telemarketers, and the Holly-Williams House in Lakeville offers a glimpse of what used to be one of the best ways to corral toddlers in a safe situation while you frolicked on your own outdoors.

Garden mazes were fairly common British backyard accessories in the 1700s, and the tradition made its way over here as well. Many schools in New England decided to let their tykes safely run off steam in mazes set up in schoolyards.

Such a maze is one of the attractions at the Holly-Williams House on Millertown Road in Lakeville (860–435–2878). Designed by toy maker Vic Reiling, this cool little labyrinth has a

A great way to keep the tots occupied.

From Monticello to a Connecticut dinner table.

nineteenth-century school bell at its center, taken from the Grove School in Salisbury. This maze appears to be composed of tall grass rather than the carefully managed hedgerows of many British mazes, but this way you can keep an eye on the wee ones' exploratory shenanigans.

While you're at the Holly-Williams House, you should also peruse an adjoining bit of greenery not far from the maze. You know him for many, many reasons, but you may not realize what a truly diverse and complicated guy Thomas Jefferson was until you meander through the garden that bears his name.

The garden may not have been tilled by Tom himself but it does feature some special species provided by the Jefferson Center for Historic Plants at Monticello. It's hard to fathom where he found the time, but Jefferson was an incredibly skilled gardener who cumulatively owned more than 10,000 acres in several locations. His interests were all over the place, yet he seemed have a preference for perennial flowers.

So do we have a little bit of Jefferson at the Holly-Williams museum? Absolutely. His legacy grows both in the influence he had on our democracy and in the cultivation of plants in this small garden. Given Mr. Jefferson's considerable intellect, will these offshoots of the plants he cultivated in time develop some type of super-intelligence and start writing declarations of independence in the dirt with their fronds? We're visiting this garden regularly to see.

The Future Is across the Street

Lakeville

Architecture is a fickle thing. One man's apple pie is another man's Brussels sprout, in a building sense. So when a really innovative, aggressive architect builds a striking structure in an area that has more traditional types of dwellings, it should come as no surprise that the collective community eyebrow raises a bit.

Or, to be a bit more blunt about it, stick some modern art in a gallery full of Old Masters and it *will* get noticed. Such is the house at 15 Beldo Road in Lakeville. Architect Alfredo de Vito caused quite a stir when he built his white house in 1985. Instead of falling into the neighborhood theme of traditional A-frame–type homes, the de Vito house looks more like an office for an ambassador from Pluto.

Sheathed in Italian marble, glass, and tile, this multilevel structure has a futuristic look that some find striking and dynamic. Other folks have been none too pleased: "People were furious when the house was built in Lakeville," explains Maura Wolf of Elyse Harney Real Estate, who is handling the house. "As I understand it, the architect built it as one of his masterpieces, yet he never actually lived in the house. It stayed empty, which made people livid. They didn't like the look of it, and here it was sitting in the middle of their neighborhood—and there

Can you believe it? Some locals actually think this house doesn't fit in with traditional New England architecture. Madness!

wasn't even anybody living in it. Somebody may have lived there at some point, but it's been empty for as long as I've been here, which is many years."

It certainly is unique, to say the least. We actually like the place, but then we've never been accused of having any taste.

But we are not alone. We're pleased to report that now the house in Lakeville has new owners, who have been actively sprucing the place up and enjoying the fascinating structure immensely. We wish them the best in their unique home.

Fast Cars in the Country

Lakeville

Back when Jim Vaill started racing an old MG around an even older lime rock pit, there wasn't much competition. Of course it was 1955, and the kids were just having fun. But then someone suggested that the ruts the young men had worn in the ground would be a good foundation for a real race track, and in this chi-chi and bucolic corner of Connecticut, Lime Rock Park was born. (But not without some heartache; construction on the track was delayed about six months after a bad flood in 1955.)

The first event was held in 1957 and attracted 6,600 people—among them Walter Cronkite, who drove a car. The track changed hands several times before racing instructor Skip Barber bought it and started a school there in 1975. He paved the track, replaced the overworked septic system, and generally turned it into a decent racing venue.

Even if he hadn't, Lime Rock is considered the prettiest track on the planet. Set in the Berkshire Mountains' foothills, Lime Rock is surrounded by farmland and Colonial houses. The nearby village of Salisbury is downright picture-postcard pretty, and if you were lucky in times past, you might have found Connecticut's favorite race driver/philanthropist/movie star there. Paul Newman, who started racing only in his late forties or thereabouts, has quite an impressive record at Lime Rock.

Lime Rock Track is at 497 Lime Rock Road, just east of Salisbury in Lakeville. Their Web site is www.limerock.com.

Dorothy's Got Nothing on Litchfield
Litchfield

Here on the windswept plains . . . OK, Connecticut doesn't have plains, but you get the idea. Here in the Berkshire hills, Dorothy would have felt right at home. This may not be Kansas, but we certainly have our own mini tornado alley. Tornadoes are surprisingly common across interior sections of southern New England. In fact, the tornado density is as great in Litchfield County as in almost any other part of the country. Statistically, about four to five tornadoes per 10,000 square miles will occur annually in Connecticut and western Massachusetts. That density of severe weather is exceeded only by Kansas and Oklahoma, which annually have between six and eight tornadoes for every 10,000 square miles.

Granted, most of our tornadoes are smallish, but they can reach the level of what occurs during the most violent of weather episodes on the Great Plains. In 1979 the devastating Windsor Locks tornado struck; ten years later, a July tornado swarm included an F–4 category tornado in Hamden with winds over 200 mph. That's a pretty big blow.

And when population density is factored into the equation, the odds of a person being affected by a tornado are greater here than any other part of the country, including Dorothy's Kansas. From 1979 to 1999 the Windsor Locks tornado was the most costly tornado to strike anywhere in the country. Our homegrown tornado lost that position to the May 1999 Oklahoma City tornado. Not that we want the record back or anything.

BOOK 'EM, DANNO

Don't you just love a happy ending to a weird story? In 1990 state police officers at Troop L barracks in Litchfield were moving from their old headquarters to a new $6 million complex.

They were leaving behind memories and a mystery—or so they thought. For as long as anyone remembered, a bullet had rested in a plaque on the old building, but no one knew how the bullet had got there. As the troopers were packing, an old man walked in and said he wanted to come clean, his conscience had been bothering him.

In World War II the old gentleman, then a young gentleman, had been drafted to fight, and his going-away party had gotten rambunctious. Yes, shots were fired. Several in fact. And well, the old man was certain his was the bullet that struck the building and left a reminder of his youthful, uh, enthusiasm and patriotism.

Would you arrest the man? Troop L officers didn't have the heart. Instead, they sent the gentleman on his way. So many years later, an arrest seemed beside the point.

You Be the Lawyer
Litchfield

It's a pretty safe bet that you've always wanted to know what it would be like to be a billionaire. And when you're not thinking about staggering amounts of cash, we bet you've been wondering what it would have been like to be a student at the first law school in the United States.

Right?

Maybe you haven't, and neither have we—until we visited the Tapping Reeve House at 82 South Street in Litchfield (860–567–4501, www.litchfieldhistoricalsociety.org/lawschool.html). We heartily recommend the experience, too.

Tapping Reeve became a lawyer the only way you could in the mid eighteenth century: by being an apprentice under a lawyer and then passing the bar. When he later became a judge, he decided to discard this tradition by starting the first real law school the country had ever seen, in Litchfield. His first pupil was Aaron Burr, who later became his brother in law.

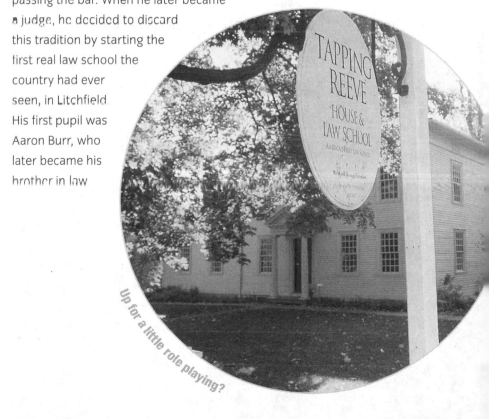

Up for a little role playing?

Today you get to "attend" the Litchfield Law School by assuming the identity of a young student (such as one Levi Woodbury) and learning about the school through his (all students then were male) eyes. You see your travel arrangements, read about your political party affiliation, write a letter home for money when you run out, and ultimately learn of your fate upon leaving school.

This is not only a neat museum, it's a great concept. It's one thing to visit a historic place that has role players but quite a different kettle of law books to play the role yourself.

A Chip off the Historical Block
Litchfield

Litchfield is a sleepy little New England town, wonderfully preserved and picturesque and clearly well looked after by its residents. But beneath the tranquil exterior, you get a sense that it's actually very important in some way. It is. It's been a hotbed for the well-to-do, the movers and shakers, and various pioneers of things like law schools and historical societies.

Here's another interesting tidbit: Going all the way back to 1856, the Litchfield Historical Society, at the corner of South and East Streets (860–567–4501), has been trying to preserve the history of the town. Even back then, these people had an unusually strong appreciation for preserving things from the past for residents of the future. You could call it an obsession, although there were certainly no designer colognes involved.

But they did like to preserve some pretty unusual, even weird, artifacts. One particularly coveted piece is the kind of thing you would find at the base of any woodpile. But this particular wood chip, encased in a beautiful little glass box, has almost a holy air about it. It's a tiny chunk of the Charter Oak, the tree that hid Connecticut's charter from the slimy hands of King James II's agents back in the 1680s.

It's odd to see such a mundane object as a chunk of wood in such a fancy display case; but then it was a very important tree that once wore this bark. The rest of the museum is full of other curious treasures, such as period clothing that you are encouraged to try on (to see if you would have fit into Litchfield's glorious past). There's also a rifle custom-built for a clergyman, which was no doubt used to encourage regular church attendance.

> Something you should know about Litchfield County: Dustin Hoffman lives here. So do Meryl Streep and Kevin Bacon. So do Susan St. James, Bill Blass, and Ralph Lauren. Yet it's very much a rural county. There are more cows than people— very well-behaved cows, but cows, nevertheless. Earl Wilson called it the "mink and manure" set.

The Devil's Second Home

New Hartford

You never really know what you're going to run into when you round a corner in this state. You could be minding your own business and suddenly get confronted by a giant ant, legions of Bernese Mountain dogs—even Satan's Kingdom.

Satan's Kingdom? No kidding. We realize that doesn't exactly sound like a place you'd want to visit, but lest you think we're talking about some sort of elevator straight to Lucifer's Lair, have no fear. We're talking about Satan's Kingdom State Recreation Area in New Hartford.

Obviously this is no Paradise Alley or Heaven's Gate, but it is a pretty, dynamic place for water sports on the West Branch of the Farmington River. This is a fantastic place for canoeists, kayakers, and tubers (and we don't mean couch potatoes). You can actually encounter some Class III rapids in these waters. Such conditions mean you might just have a hell of a good time shooting the river (sorry about that).

So why the diabolical name? It is widely reported that in the 1700s the rugged area around the gorge just outside New Hartford was largely peopled with criminals, miscreants, ne'er-do-wells, and probably trolls and ogres (although we haven't seen such a declaration about those last two in any texts). The name Satan's Kingdom was allegedly coined by local clergy, who believed the place was a virtual no-man's-land, an isolated area that was wild and lawless. Now it's just a great place to recreate.

Fear not the name.

The Oceanless Lighthouse

New Hartford

It's always enlightening to realize that your perceptions have been limited by the narrow prism of your own experience. Case in point: We always assumed that lighthouses were huge, towerlike structures erected near reefs and other maritime hazards to help mariners navigate around them. Given this definition, you would think that any story about a lighthouse would be somehow associated with Connecticut's rugged coastline.

But in typical Nutmeg fashion, some of our resident ancestors decided to create a different type of lighthouse many years ago, when a small community was settled not far from New Hartford, in the area now known as the People's State Forest. The official name of the settlement was Barkhamsted Lighthouse, and most historians believe it was started with the unlikely pairing (at the time) of a Wethersfield girl named Molly Barber and a Native American named Chaugham in the 1770s. The community that grew up on this site was a diverse one that included recently freed slaves, newly arrived Europeans, and various indigenous folks. The village thrived all the way through the 1850s.

Why was it called a lighthouse? The story goes that the lights from this small town served as a navigational beacon in the night for stagecoaches on their way to New Hartford. Aha! Much as camels are called ships of the desert, stagecoaches were at one time the ships of the Connecticut wilderness. Today you can see vestiges of the Lighthouse community off the Jessie Gerard Trail in People's State Forest, just off the East River Road.

The Mysterious Green Theater
Norfolk

You drive by the building on Route 44 and it really jumps out at you. Actually, it grabs you and shakes you and screams in your face, "I AM THEATER! ATTEND ME!"

Well, maybe it doesn't scream, but the light green hue and unusual architecture really get your attention—and they should. The Greenwood Theater in Norfolk (860–542–0026) is an unusual building where unusual plays and musicals for today are performed—and actors refuse to use microphones.

"We believe in classical theater without electronic aids and true quality through writing and performance alone," declares the theater's co-owner and producer, Maura Cavanagh. "This theater was designed for this. I'm not really sure if it was looking for us or we were looking for it. It's a writer's theater, and we're writers."

Where microphones are considered a form of technical contamination.

Cavanagh and her associates took this badly dilapidated theater and in less than two years gave it a new lease on life. In the process they discovered that they had a very unusual building, with clear Japanese influence in some of the carvings and ornaments that seemed out of place for the period. Further research revealed a mystery: They couldn't find out who actually designed the building. This was very curious indeed, especially since the theater had been a fixture in the town and a source of entertainment and community activities for so long.

"It's really quite a puzzle," admits Cavanagh. "One very credible theory is that the building was based on a standardized plan that was common during the period. Each town had to have what was then called an opera house for a variety of functions. It's possible it was a blue plate special of the day architecturally."

Regardless of who originally built the theater, it's now a thriving venue for the arts and once again a source of entertainment in this small community—just as it was more than a hundred years ago. It's also a great place just to visit and admire.

Some Enchanted Diner

North Canaan

If you were a small lunch counter, or even just a hot-dog cart, and you wanted to be a diner when you grew up, one amazing eatery should be your role model: the Collin's Diner in North Canaan (860–824–7040, www.collinsdiner.com).

This is a diner's diner—a cool eatery that is like no other on the planet because no other diner has more history, longevity, or "train cred." Train cred is of course short for train credibility, as opposed to street credibility, because this diner has come a long way to be here (from another state, in fact) and has always been a stone's throw from a train station. The station itself was built in 1870 and was recently gutted by fire, but the town is hoping to rebuild.

The Collin's Diner was built in New Jersey and opened here on August 11, 1941. It is filled with unique fixtures, such as the marble in the counter, which was liberated from a broken-down bar in Texas. So what we have here is a sixty-year-old Connecticut diner, built in Jersey, with some Lone Star marble. Yee-haw!

Like the quality of the food and service, owner Mohammed Abo-Hamzy has tried to keep the diner located at Routes 44 and 7 as original as possible, right down to the handles on the refrigerators. "Only three things aren't original," he says: "the soda machine, as we used to keep the sodas in an iced-down sink, the coffee machine, and me."

This well-traveled diner is as eclectic as it is historic.

Probably no other diner in America has been in more commercials, movies, and other media, and it's safe to say that few establishments have a more loyal following. A New Haven motorcycle club whose members love to make the trip up to the Litchfield hills even gave an award to the Collin's Diner for years of great food and friendship. It's rare to see such loyalty to an eatery, but once you chat with Mohammed and hear his devotion to the place and its customers—and soak up the atmosphere and eat great chow—you can see why it's downright magical. These days, the day-to-day running of the diner is handled by Mohammed's son Ameen and the rest of the family, who are dedicated to keeping the place that has meant so much to so many largely unchanged. Ameen is even more famous as a poet, and each summer since 1995 a Poetry is Music gathering has been held at the diner. It grows in popularity every season.

If These Stones Could Talk

Salisbury

Connecticut is big on its dead, and Ruth Shapleigh-Brown is executive director of Connecticut Gravestone Network—a volunteer group that protects historical burial grounds and cemeteries like Dutcher's Burying Ground in Salisbury. She and others travel around the state clearing brush, taking down information from stones almost lost to the elements, and making sure the plots are protected from development.

Along with the information on the stones, the network also records the histories of the various burying grounds. Dutcher's was purchased by the town of Salisbury in 1802 from Rulff Dutcher, for $1.00. The earliest graves found here date from 1767, and the latest gravestone is dated 1881. Carvings on many of the stones are all but eaten away, and people like Shapleigh-Brown discourage "rubbings"—placing thin paper over the stones and then rubbing a pencil across in order to see what the stone once said. Even that tends to wear down the already-fragile brownstones and limestones.

The cemetery is a good example of many of the 2,400 cemeteries scattered around Connecticut. (The last accurate count taken was in 1934, by the Work Projects Administration.) Within Dutcher's, there are the family plots—like those of the Carter family, with matriarch Anna Carter's stone calling her the "relief" of husband Benoni, who is buried next to her. Take a moment to read the stones. Anna Carter must have left suddenly. A poem carved into the foot of her 4-foot-high stone reads:

> *When Death is sent from God above*
> *And calls us from those who dearly love*
> *He doesn't always warning give*
> *Dear friends, be careful how you live.*

Dutcher's Burying Ground is on Route 44, heading west just past the Housatonic River and up Weatogue Road on your right.

Some of Connecticut's early settlers are buried here.

THERE'S NO SUCH THING AS "JUST A CHAIR"

And don't you think otherwise, bub. For nearly 200 years, the Hitchcock Chair Company turned out distinctive hardwood furniture from an 11,000-square foot factory in New Hartford. At its peak the company had around one hundred employees.

Initially, founder Lambert Hitchcock (1795–1852) manufactured individual chair parts that he sold as DIY kits. Later, he sold complete factory-made chairs typically painted black or red with stenciled decoration. The seats were not upholstered but caned.

Today, Hitchcock chairs are included in many a museum's collection of American decorative arts.

Learn More Than You Thought Possible
at the Tavern Museum

Simsbury

That's the Phelps Tavern Museum, where you can see what it was like
to belly up, colonial style. Be prepared to lose some illusions. People
who want to believe there were lusty barmaids waiting at your beck
and call can just forget about it. Taverns and inns, such as the one
housed in the historic Captain Elisha Phelps House, were usually part of
private homes, and innkeepers were mostly married. So things were a
lot tamer than you might think.

The Phelps was home to three generations of tavernkeepers, from
1786 to 1849, and was the site of ordination balls and Masonic meetings, among other gatherings. If it's a special occasion, the museum will
have on display the Higley copper, an ingenious local currency first
minted by Samuel Higley, a doctor who trained at Yale University. The
first coin was originally valued at three pence, but townspeople said
that was too much, so Higley, who mined iron on a 143-acre site in what
is now East Granby, stamped "Value me as you please" on the coin. It
was never officially sanctioned, and only a few authentic coins remain.
To visit the museum, take Route 10 (Hopmeadow Road) to Simsbury, or
call (860) 658–2500. The Web site is www.simsburyhistory.org.

George Washington Didn't Lunch Here—But He Could Have

Simsbury

Not far from a steel bridge on Route 185, a tree that's roughly 350 years old (maybe older) holds the title of "Largest Tree in the State." At least, no bigger specimens have stepped up to steal the crown. It may also be the largest sycamore in New England. Again, no other takers have arrived to say otherwise.

The sycamore, named the Gifford Pinchot, has had seeds removed for propagation at America's Historic Forests in Des Moines, Iowa, where seeds from other famous and historic trees also have children growing.

Pinchot was a Simsbury native who died in 1964 at the age of ninety-nine, and was the first head of the U.S. Forestry Service and cofounder of the Yale School of Forestry.

The Pinchot stands almost 100 feet tall, with a branch-to-branch span of roughly 140 feet. It can be found just off Route 185 on the east bank of the Farmington River.

If this isn't the largest tree in the state, then we don't know our trees.

The German Spy Who Wasn't

Simsbury

Just before America's involvement in World War I, businessman Gilbert Heublein completed construction of a tower that, sitting atop a ridge on Talcott Mountain, rose 1,000 feet above sea level. The tower was a replacement for one first built in 1810 by Daniel Wadsworth on his estate, Monte Video. That tower lasted until 1840 and was replaced by another one that burned in 1864. A third tower was built a few years later, and it lasted until 1889.

Proud that he was continuing a towering tradition, Heublein threw a party to celebrate. To show off the tower and his summer estate's gardens, he lit the mountain as it had never been lit before.

But these were war times, and at midnight several uniformed police officers arrived on the estate. Seems they suspected Heublein of using the lights to pass information to German spies. Heublein, a true-blue American, was mortified. He offered his summer home as a possible training ground for American troops. The government never took him up on his offer, but he never forgot the night the lights brought the law. The tower, which is open in warmer months, is accessible by a 1-mile trail off Talcott Mountain Road.

Padlocks of the Ancient Ones

Terryville

If you told someone you had traveled a great distance to see a baroque lock, they might ask if you would be likewise interested in viewing a damaged tool box or malfunctioning toaster oven.

But this time we're talking about baroque as in Baroque, the dominant style in Europe around the seventeenth and eighteenth centuries. The Lock Museum is one of those weird and wonderful places where commonplace objects take on a whole new dimension. Did you know that the basic design for the tumbler lock dates back thousands of years? This museum even has an Egyptian lock to show how thieves were deterred back when home security meant you owned a large club or, like Pharaoh, had some particularly well-trained cats.

This museum at 230 Main Street (860–589–6359) has probably the world's most comprehensive collection of locks of every size and description, manufactured by such famous names as Mosler, Reese, Slaymaker, Sesamee, and Slage. There are regular padlocks, push-button combination locks, and even an enormous lock from an English castle. Locks don't just mean the external variety, either, for there are plenty of doorknobs with integral locks from such storied venues as the Waldorf Astoria Hotel. These are not just devices designed to keep maids out of your room early in the morning; they're small works of architectural art. In fact, most big hotels like the Waldorf made the lock companies destroy the patterns once they had finished installing the locks in the hotel to ensure that no other building would have the same design. Neat stuff.

Got keys?

Celluloid Gets Real

Torrington

You've got to admire the survival skills of Bugs Bunny. He's been around for more than half a century and looks as young as ever. He's definitely a senior citizen, but he's still got class and staying power that are the envy of animated rodents worldwide. He's learned to adapt over time and has always found a way to appeal to an audience. The Warner Theatre in Torrington (860–489–7180; www.warnertheatre.org) has also found a way to survive—by adopting the art form it was designed to replace. Built by the Warner Brothers (the nutty guys who brought Bugs to the world) in 1931, the theater ushered in (pun intended) an era of the motion picture as the replacement to live theater. One thousand and eight hundred seats were surrounded by stunning Art Deco and even an enormous chandelier.

You won't see Star Wars here . . . unless somebody makes it into a play, that is.

But over time the Warner itself came under attack. First the flood of 1955 nearly ruined the magnificent building, then divestment saw the theater sold, and then bankruptcy almost saw the classic building demolished. But the people of Connecticut refused to let the theater die, and a successful campaign was mounted to buy and restore the Warner.

In an ironic quirk of fate, the kind of entertainment that the Warner was built to supplant has saved it from ruin. Now this beautiful building is the home of plays, concerts, musical recitals, Chinese acrobats, and community events fueled by living, breathing actors (and an occasional movie or two). Not a bad legacy for such a resilient structure; I think Bugs Bunny, showrabbit that he is, would definitely approve.

The Old Gray Mare
Washington

Sick and lame horses would be a seller's worst nightmare, but the H.O.R.S.E. farm of Washington is different. In the twenty-five years that volunteers have been taking in bag-of-bones horses, the people at H.O.R.S.E., the Humane Organization Representing Suffering Equines, have retrained abused and neglected horses and prepared them for new homes. People say they work miracles, and sometimes the rescuers would be inclined to agree. The farm uses the latest in veterinary care and hours and hours of volunteer time. They have a vet and an acupuncturist, as well.

On the farm, horses that should have been dead are pampered and retrained and brought back to life. The farm has also been known to take in cats, dogs—and the occasional human who needs a place to unwind. The H.O.R.S.E. Farm is at Wilbur Road in Washington. Call (860) 868–1960 for more information or to volunteer—or to adopt a horse—or visit them at www.horseofct.org.

Connecticut's state song, "Yankee Doodle," was first sung, according to recent scholarship, during the French and Indian War as a taunt to the ragtag militia. But the lyrics are far older, stretching back to the 1600s. The Dutch may have come up with the nickname "Yankee," the approximate equivalent of "country squire," or somewhere thereabouts. New Englanders hated the song, and singing it could spark a fistfight. But by the battles of Lexington and Concord, the new Americans were singing the song in defiance as the whipped British retreated. The tune so enraged British troops that part of the terms of surrender at Yorktown was that the American bands would not play "Yankee Doodle." When the British troops marched down a column of French and American soldiers, however, they kept their heads turned to the French as an insult to the Americans. Angry, the Marquis de Lafayette ordered the musicians to strike up—you guessed it—"Yankee Doodle."

Say "Bridge!"
West Cornwall

The covered bridge at West Cornwall is one of the state's three picturesque covered bridges (and one of America's maybe 1,000), and it may be the most popular. Every Columbus Day, townspeople hold Covered Bridge Days with fly-fishing demonstrations, samples of local food, and a chance to win stoneware from Cornwall Bridge Pottery. The event attracts people from all over New England—even from Vermont, where they have covered bridges of their own.

Even when the party balloons aren't popping, the one-lane bridge is often backed up—with photographers, if not cars. The bridge, which crosses the cascading Housatonic River, is an extremely popular subject for shutterbugs, who often think little of blocking traffic while they get just the right angle—like standing in the middle of the road to shoot down the long bridge itself. We know people who've done that.

In addition to being on the walls and in the scrapbooks of photographers near and far, the bridge has been featured on Connecticut state lottery tickets. Not bad for a bridge built in 1864. And it has at times moved poets to wax, well, poetic:

I'm just a covered bridge, that's all
For years in this place I've stood;
Can some wish for my downfall,
Because I'm made of wood!

OK. We didn't say it was *good* poetry. By the way, do not be confused with Cornwall Bridge, the town. That's farther south on Route 7. You want West Cornwall, at the intersections of Routes 7 and 128.

This kind of picture-pretty place really does exist in Connecticut. No, really.

NORTH—CENTRAL

MASSACHUSETTS

Enfield

Windsor Locks

East Windsor

Windsor

East Hartford

Manchester

West Hartford

Hartford

Farmington

Newington

Bristol

New Britain

0   10 Miles

0   10 KM

NORTH-CENTRAL

The Carousel Time Capsule
Bristol

There are people out there—and you may be one of them—who are scared to death of clowns. There's something about their smiling, painted faces that seems surreal to the point of evil, a cheeriness that masks ugliness behind thick coats of makeup.

Would you believe that there are individuals who feel the same way about the horses on carousels? We kid you not; a dear friend of ours is one of them.

Or *was*, we should say. But something very curious, and wonderful, happened when she visited the New England Carousel Museum in Bristol (860–585–5411, www.thecarouselmuseum.org). We figured we were in trouble when we waltzed through the door and heard the familiar strains of carousel pipe music. Our associate felt a special kind of fear, which she described as like being locked in a Fellini movie capped with the frightening ending of Hitchcock's *Strangers on a Train* rushing up to spite her.

As it turned out, this museum cured her fear of carousels and gave her (and us) a whole new appreciation for the art that goes into them. The pivotal moment was seeing a carousel horse carved by Marcus Illions—a wooden steed created to commemorate the release of the Lincoln-head penny in 1909. Like all other carousel horses (be they standers, prancers, or jumpers), it's composed of more than seventy pieces of wood and is absolutely beautiful to gaze upon.

This museum takes you through the history of such amazing horses (and the odd pig, camel, and carousel giraffe), explains the labor involved in restoration, and even shares the secret of treasures found in the hollow bellies of many a restored carousel horse. This space turns out to be a very singular type of time capsule, for over time (and countless rides by fair visitors), items fall through the pole space and are preserved here. Not only do such wonders help eliminate any fears you may have of carousel horses, they are icing on the cake of a trip through a special world we rarely get to see anymore.

And you thought I was just a make-believe horse.

It's about Time

Bristol

First things first: If you are Quasimodo, or have an aversion to things that tick, buzz, or gong on occasion, you should perhaps avoid the American Clock and Watch Museum at 100 Maple Street in Bristol (860–583–6070, www.clockmuseum.org). There are all manner of time-keeping devices here, and they have all kinds of noisy ways to notify the world that time, in fact, is marching on.

But if (unlike the famous hunchback) you're not tormented by "The Bells!" and you've ever been curious about the scope of timekeeping devices and where they all came from, this is your Mecca.

Why are all these clocks and watches here in Bristol, ticking, buzzing and, on occasion, gonging? Why did literally thousands of timekeeping devices decide to flee their owners and congregate here, in the historic Miles Lewis house?

Simple. Years ago Connecticut was a world hub for watch and clock manufacturing. While this formidable collection has timekeeping devices from all over the world, the bulk of these clocks and watches come not just from New England but from Connecticut itself. For nearly fifty years this museum has been collecting timepieces and now possesses more than 1,400 specimens.

From tiny key watches to a Porky Pig wrist timepiece (for p-p-p-p-punctuality) to massive tower clocks, there's something here for just about anybody who enjoys mechanical devices. The collection is here; all you need is the time.

The Country's Oldest Continuously Operated Amusement Park

Bristol

In 1846, a Bristol scientist conducted what was advertised as "a series of beautiful experiments in electricity," and attracted a crowd at Lake Compounce. The experiments failed, but the crowds inspired the land's owner to set up picnic tables and organize lakeside concerts. (Entertainment was cheap in New England in those days.)

And Lake Compounce was born. Over time, a restaurant was built, then a carousel and a ballroom, which hosted the up-and-coming Frank Sinatra. Rides were added, and Lake Compounce reigned supreme in the post–World War II years. Families from all over New England took their little baby boomers for a look at the Cowboy Caravan.

But like many amusement parks, Lake Compounce fell

Perhaps the sign should say OPEN IN PERPETUITY.

on hard times in the '80s, and sometimes heroic measures were taken to hang on to that "continuously" part of their advertisement.

But in recent years, the park has grown and expanded. They've managed to thrive, in fact, and their Boulder Dash roller coaster received the highest rating by the National Amusement Park Historical Association in the first year of its operation in 2000.

The park is just off exit 31 on I-84 in Bristol. For more information, visit www.lakecompounce.com.

Birding at the Old Meat Town
East Hartford

Years ago a marshy bog just off I–384 in East Hartford was the site of a huge slaughterhouse and butcher shop. Local residents called the area "Meat Town," and the name, for the most part, stuck. (Simple nicknames are the best, aren't they?)

Today the slaughterhouse is gone, the butcher shop is closed down, and—oddly—all that remains is one of the state's best-kept secrets among bird lovers. The eleven or so acres, which look strangely out of place for a strip by an interstate highway, have become a haven for unusual and generally migratory birds. So it has also become the hangout for unusual bird lovers, as well.

Representatives from the National Audubon Society swear by the land for the multiple sightings it's yielded. In a state heavily populated by bird-watchers, many of whom prefer the simpler term "birders," Meat Town is the place to be. You may find yellow-headed blackbirds, which usually don't migrate farther east than Illinois, or the rare peregrine falcons, or graceful herons.

Want to bird with the best of them? Take I–384 to exit 1, Silver Lane. Go west on Silver Lane to Rolling Meadow Drive, and follow it until it becomes Lombardo. Meat Town is—or was—in this general area.

AIRPORT TRANSPORTATION THAT DIDN'T FLY

Ah, what might have been! Many's the time we encounter things that sure look like they were great ideas, only to find out they didn't exactly "fly."

A perfect example of this is found at the Connecticut Trolley Museum in East Windsor (860–627–6540; www.ct-trolley.org). Sitting outside, right next to the parking lot, are three futuristic train cars—sort of like a monorail that escaped its track and stopped in the weeds. The sides of these chic (but weathered) transports read Bradley International. Say what? If, like us, you've been flying in and out of this airport for years, how come we never got to ride in one of these cool, futuristic trains?

We shouldn't feel bad, because basically nobody did.

"The system was initially put in by one governor in the 1970s, and then another governor came in and didn't like it," explains Warren Stannard, Bradley's supervising airport engineer. "It was used a few times but never actually operated in an official capacity for passengers. A station out by where the current cargo facilities are came into the terminal, and there were a few turns in the track. It wasn't really a long-distance type of a thing."

Why the program was scrapped by the Ella Grasso administration is still subject to debate, and some say it was just a matter of making room for a new, larger terminal down the road. Others say politics was involved. But the cars (which came from the Ford Motor Company, as did the computer) were pulled off the tracks before the train ever really got going and were kept in a garage. Years later, the tracks themselves were destroyed when a new terminal was built in 1985. The massive computer that ran the system (remember when computers were the size of a four-car garage?) was demolished as well, even though the airport tried to donate it to UConn and other institutions before it was bulldozed into rubble.

"Man, that thing was built well," comments Stannard on the futuristic train line. "I felt kind of bad in some respects when we tore it down, because I think it could have made the system work."

These cool little trains were once ahead of their time.

Sphere of Effluence
East Windsor

It's huge, red, and has a certain mechanical randomness to it. In fact, when you first look at it, you might think either something really weird is going on or you've encountered a work in progress.

"Perhaps," you say to yourself, "this particular fire truck is undergoing restoration, and part of the engine has been ripped out and placed on the front bumper to make it easier to work on."

A big silver ball on top of this naked engine creates even more speculation. The backyard chef in you decides there's a Weber Grill mounted on the front of this truck to facilitate on-site barbecues after the fire has been put out. Your scientific side decides that someone obviously mounted a small planetarium on the vehicle to entertain schoolchildren when they tour the firehouse.

But what you're actually looking at is a vintage piece of fire-fighting gear, and this 1929 Ahrens-Fox Pumper truck is just as it should be. This style of truck mounted the piston-powered water pump on the bumper in front of the engine, and the massive metal sphere is just a pressure-equalizing device to help smooth out the pump pulses. Without it, water would flow through the hose inconsistently and be much more difficult to control.

Such classic engineering marvels are a common sight at the Connecticut Fire Museum in East Windsor (860–623–4732, www.ct-trolley .org/Firemuseum/), on the grounds of the Connecticut Trolley Museum. Not to be confused with the Fire Museum in Manchester, this facility focuses on fire trucks, and they have a wild assortment of vintage machines. In addition to Ahrens-Fox, you'll see trucks from Zabek, Seagrave, Buffalo, American-LaFrance, Mack, Peter Pirsch, and others. Weird, wild, and wonderfully unusual, this place will entertain motorheads and nonmotorheads alike.

It looks like this fire truck crashed into a planetarium!

A WHOLE LOT OF SHAKIN' GOING ON

In the mid-eighteenth century a British woman, Ann Lee, founded a Protestant sect known as the Shakers—so called because of their ritualized twitching during worship services. The sect quickly took root in the New World in utopian communities from Kentucky to Ohio to Maine.

Members believed in heaven on earth through an orderly kind of living that included celibacy. Married couples who joined the sect together understood they would live in separate living quarters as brother and sister. Shakers kept the pews packed with converts, the destitute who had no place else to go, and orphans left with the community.

Shakers came to Enfield, north of Hartford, and established a community that at its height boasted five villages—called families—and 260 members, who settled into one hundred stately buildings on prime farmland. This particular group is thought to have been the first manufacturers of packaged seeds in the country. But attracting members to an obscure, sexless group grew too difficult. During World War I, the Enfield community disbanded and its remaining members moved to other Shaker villages. The bulk of the old community now lies on the grounds of a Connecticut prison, but several large, white barnlike buildings remain and can be seen from Shaker Road (Route 220).

Washington against the Wall

Enfield

It's not very often that you think about the historical value of wallpaper. Other home furnishings, like antiques, sure. But wallpaper? It's that terrible stuff that peels when you need it to stick, sticks to things it shouldn't (like your assistant, when you're installing it), and is generally a pain to deal with when it gets old and fragile.

But the Martha Parsons House in Enfield (860-745-6064) has some wallpaper that is not only historically important but pretty dang durable as well. It has been gracing the entry hall of this beautiful home for roughly 200 years and is believed to be the only George Washington Memorial Wallpaper to still be on the original walls where it was installed. It's quite solemn and classic in appearance and was designed (as Michael Miller's excellent book on Enfield recalls the original advertisement) "to perpetuate the memory of the best of men."

DO NOT allow your cat to sharpen his claws on this wallpaper.

The wallpaper itself was recently removed, cleaned, and treated (a job that boggles the mind) and then reinstalled, and it is a highlight to this wonderfully preserved dwelling. But there's so much more to this house, because Miss Parsons wanted to preserve this slice of early New England life for the citizens of Enfield to visit. Several lifetimes of furnishings passed from generation to generation are on display, and the story of the final occupant is a fascinating study of a strong, independent woman living in a time where such unconventionality was discouraged. There's also the intrigue of the name of the house: It was originally built to house ministers, also known as parsons. It ended up providing a home for Parsons—a formidable woman with a deep sense of community rather than a man of the cloth.

Be It Ever So Crumbly
Farmington

In 1987, a real estate mogul named Ben Sisti built a $2.3 million, fifty-two room house in Farmington. Usually mansions in Connecticut aren't that big a deal, but this one came complete with a nightclub, one hundred telephone extension lines, a twenty-eight-station workout room, twenty television screens in one wall, five kitchens, and a fake waterfall. Oh, and an indoor shooting range.

So this one caught the eye of even the most hidebound of Yankees.

Sadly, Sisti built his chateau with dirty money and, as a partner in a corrupt realty company, he was forced to change addresses. He's now serving jail time for cheating clients out of millions of dollars.

And his dream house? It's changed hands a couple of times, from a Lithuanian businessman to, more recently, boxer Mike Tyson, who bought it in 1996 for $2.8 million.

Something about the house, however, is not suitable. After roughly a week of enjoying the splendor, Tyson—who's had his own run-ins with the law—put the thing on the market for $5 million.

In 2003, rap artist 50 Cent (who was born Curtis James Jackson III) bought it from an ex-wife of Tyson's for $4.1 million.

See the house (but not the rapper) at 46 Poplar Bars Road in Farmington.

Not Your Mama's Chandelier
Hartford

Underneath a 14-foot-long, 8-foot-wide, massive, misshapen orange-red column of fire, champagne glasses clink together and well-dressed docents mingle.

Well, not real fire. Instead, it's *Ode to Joy*, glass artist Dale Chihuly's much-talked-about creation for the Bushnell Center for the Performing Arts in Hartford. The unusual light was part of a $45 million expansion project, and it can be viewed in the historic theater's Autorino Great Hall.

The space beneath *Ode* has become one of *the* gathering places in Connecticut's capital city, for where else could you stare straight up into fire?

Chihuly, a Seattle-based artist, has been called the Picasso of glass, which is odd given that glass nearly killed him. In a 1976 car accident, Chihuly flew straight through a car windshield, lost the use of his left eye and gained 253 stitches. Before the accident—and a later one he suffered while sailing—Chihuly was a glass-blower. Now he's an over-seer of glass-blowers and a designer.

There's another chandelier similar to *Ode* in England, and Chihuly built a bridge of glass in Salt Lake City that was dedicated during the 2002 Olympic winter games.

Ode to Joy is not Connecticut's only Chihuly. Another, a five-ton blue-and-white glass cascade sculpture, is just down Route 2 at the Mohegan Sun casino, and there's another in Norwalk at Ocean Drive restaurant.

But Would You Belong to a Club That Would Have the Likes of You?

Hartford

As long as there have been people, there have been people who are better than you, or at least think they are. New York has elite clubs. So does Boston. Why not Hartford?

By the turn of the nineteenth century, Connecticut's capital had its Hartford Female Beneficent Society, its Hartford Arts Union, and its Sons of Temperance. But it is the Hartford Club that sustains.

The Hartford Club is lowering its standards— even the likes of you can eat here now.

This oh-so-exclusive enclave was formed in 1873 as a site for "gentle-men who had agreed to form an Association for the promotion of social intercourse, art, and literature." This during the economic Panic of 1873, which Hartford weathered nicely, thank you.

Through the years the place has been home to some famous Connecticut names. The group first met in the old Trumbull House, home of Joseph Trumbull, nephew of a former state governor and a former (inept) governor himself. Later they moved to the former Wadsworth mansion (near the current Wadsworth Atheneum), where George Washington's horse once slept in the barn out back. No kidding.

It hasn't been all hoity-toity. In 1881 Samuel L. Clemens—aka author Mark Twain—was elected to the club. He'd first come to Hartford in 1868 to arrange for the publication of his *Innocents Abroad,* and he liked what he saw. He wrote to a friend, "I tell you I have to walk mighty straight. I desire to have the respect of this sterling old Puritan community . . . so I don't dare to smoke after I go to bed, & in fact, I don't dare to do anything that's comfortable and natural." He livened things up just a bit.

If you're not a member, see if you can cadge an invitation to lunch at the club at 46 Prospect. It's loosened its cravat just a tinge.

A Bucolic Retreat
Hartford

In 1812 the Connecticut State Medical Society met to discuss the plight of the mentally ill. From that meeting the Institute of Living—then less poetically called the Hartford Retreat for the Insane—received a state charter in 1822. It was Connecticut's first hospital and one of the country's first mental hospitals. It specialized in what was then called "moral treatment." Patients were put in a bucolic setting of rare trees and flowers in a campus protected from city life by a tall, brick wall.

In the 1860s the grounds were redone by no less than Frederick Law Olmstead, a Hartford native who also designed New York City's Central Park. Before long the lovely grounds became a good place for Hollywood starlets to dry out—or hide out. The Institute, at 400 Washington, continues today as part of Hartford Hospital.

The Black Bag Retirement Home
Hartford

In the good old days, you could always identify a physician by his or her little black bag, right? When placed on your kitchen table this often scuffed and weathered minisuitcase meant, "Yes, I make house calls, and, yes, there's something in this bag that will make you feel better." We know what happened to house calls, but what the heck happened to those charming little valises?

Apparently a great number of them retired to Hartford.

We say this because there is a large assortment of little black bags distributed through the Menczer Museum of Medicine and Dentistry in Hartford (860–236–5613, http://library.uchc.edu/hms/menczer.html), located in the headquarters of the Hartford Medical Society. Inside a fairly boring brick building lies the extraordinary history of medicine in this country, as told by the equipment that physicians have devised over the years to cure, heal, and confuse the billing people at your neighborhood HMO.

Exhibits range from a nineteenth-century medical journal (which includes conditions like heartburn, described as "a painful sensation of heat or upper acrimony at particular times, about the upper orifice of the stomach") to some pretty horrific antique medical hardware. A lot of the tools look as though they were designed more to *inflict* pain than to relieve it, but in the hands of a skilled physician they could work miracles. Or, in the hands of Dr. Robert Listen, they could remove a diseased limb as well as two fingers off his assistant, who didn't get out of his way fast enough.

Other interesting items include a variety of optometrist's machines, several complete dentist's stations (with spit sinks that would no doubt impress experts on the *Antiques Road Show*), and a 1911 X-ray machine that looks as though it might have generated a "death ray" that no doubt would have caused problems for Buck Rogers. All in all, a very wild ride for doctors and patients alike.

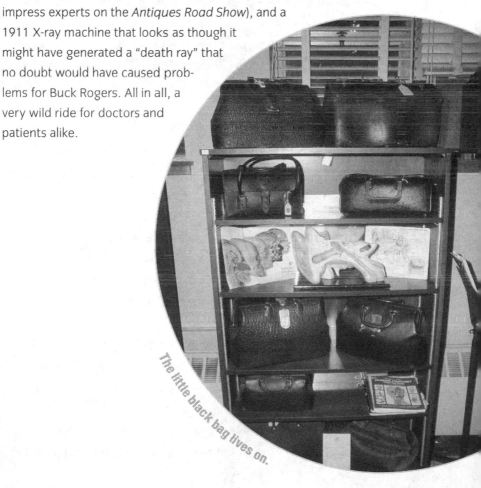

The little black bag lives on.

THE MISSING GOVERNOR

Oh, what a strange and curious animal is Connecticut politics! As you know from this very tome, with many scandals and scandalettes the last several years, we have been burdened with the nickname *Corrupticut*. A good chunk of this rather unseemly reputation has come from the activities of a certain former governor, who is now a convicted felon.

This brings us to a rather curious situation that recently befell our state, involving the three-way collision of art, tradition, and politics. As in most states, it is customary to have a portrait made of a departing governor to hang on the wall of a public building (in our case the State Library's Museum of Connecticut History). This way a citizen can view all the state's former chief executives as they pose on canvas in a dignified manner. Makes sense, right? So how could such a time-honored custom become controversial?

Well, things got ugly when Governor John G. Rowland had to resign from office, and then pled guilty to a felony count of corruption that resulted in jail time. The question was raised about the portrait, and there was a bit of a snit by state residents who cried foul. They didn't think it appropriate for state money to be used to immortalize a governor who committed crimes in office that resulted in his incarceration, even though before that point he had been elected to multiple terms and was (for a while at least) pretty popular. Understandable.

Things looked to be in a logjam until we encountered the Strange Case of the Missing Portrait. Connecticut artist Robert Sibold watched the portrait debate with interest, and then decided to chime in. You see, Mr. Sibold knew there was already a portrait of Rowland because he had painted it in 1996. This would seem to solve a problem, because if the picture already existed the state wouldn't have to pony up the cash to have one done and it could be displayed with a minimum of economic controversy. The thing is, Sibold had no clue what had happened to it.

"I had no idea where it was," Sibold told the *Manchester Journal Inquirer*'s Tom Breen. "As far as I knew, Governor Rowland owned it."

As is often the case, something that was missing was actually in plain view in a public place. Rowland's portrait was "discovered" hanging on the wall in Eolia, the mansion at Harkness Memorial State Park outside of Waterford. State Librarian Kendall F. Wiggin had the portrait moved to the Museum of Connecticut History in the State Library in Hartford, where it is now displayed with the other governors (the vast majority of whom are not convicted felons). As for who actually paid for the portrait to begin with, it is still being kept under wraps.

Picture, picture on the wall, which is the crookedest of them all?

A Home for Huck
Hartford

It's hard to say whether it most resembles a riverboat or a chocolate factory, but Mark Twain's Hartford home on Farmington Avenue (860–247–0998, www.marktwainhouse.org) is a bizarre structure. Designed by architect Edward Potter (no relation to Harry, as far as we know), the place is a wild, warm, intriguing residence as complex as the man himself. As if mimicking his wild, unruly hair, there are chimneys sprouting everywhere and no fewer than five balconies. A now-defunct local paper, the *Hartford Daily Times*, wrote an apt description of the place in the 1870s:

Riverboat meets chocolate factory.

"Many of the readers of *The Times,* doubtless, have had at least an external view of the structure, which already has acquired something beyond local fame; and such persons, we think, will agree with us in the opinion that it is one of the oddest looking buildings in the state ever designed for a dwelling, if not in the whole country."

Twain and his family lived in the house from 1874 to 1891, and early on, the endless building process wore the famous writer's patience a bit thin. According to Albert Paine's biography, Twain complained:

"I have been bullyragged by the builder, by his foreman, by the architect, by the tapestry devil who is to upholster the furniture, by the idiot who is putting down the carpets, by the scoundrel who is setting up the billiard table (and has left the balls in New York), by the wildcat who is sodding the ground and finishing the driveway (after the sun went down), by a book agent, whose body is in the backyard and the coroner notified. Just think of this going on the whole day long, and I loathe details with all my heart!"

There's no home on earth quite like it, and excellent tours are given for a modest fee.

The Egging of Politics
Hartford

Ah, the institutions of higher learning! Where else can you find the dialogues of Plato, the latest in computer-aided engineering methods, and an ostrich egg with a little diorama of the Iran-Contra scandal inside it?

Maybe not all college campuses have that last item but the University of Hartford does, in its collection of artifacts of American political life (www.hartford.edu/plmus/exhibits.html). This eclectic assemblage of memorabilia from America's electoral history provides peerless insight into political expression, from the ornate uniforms worn by partisans in political rallies to some really odd campaign goodies (like an Abraham Lincoln meerschaum pipe or a pack of Adlai Stevenson cigarettes).

From women's suffrage to the relationship of the press to the presidency, substantial collections cover substantial issues like no other museum you'll find anywhere. The complexity, controversy, and creativity of political campaigns is explained through artifacts from elections past, and the scope of the material is truly impressive.

And then there are Barbara Frye's incredible ostrich eggs. Like rogue Fabergé eggs that somehow left their owners and discovered politics, her artistic collection celebrates significant political events with small displays inside the shells that you really have to see to believe. These eggs could have become enormous omelets, but instead they're a bizarre and interesting tribute to our political system, warts and all.

Until you've seen this diorama of the Iran-Contra scandal, you've never really experienced politics Connecticut-style.

The complete collection is not on full display at this writing, but is residing in the Mortensen Library archives (860–768–4264 ext. 4268). Give them a call to examine the artifacts until they are put back on display, hopefully in the near future.

And Now This: A Word from the Great Beyond
Hartford

The younger and more eccentric sister of author Harriet Beecher Stowe, Isabella Beecher Hooker combined all the elements of her time to create in her Forest Street home (now privately owned and divided into apartments) a combination salon and rolling séance.

Isabella, a suffragist, was also a spiritualist and used her home for multiple meetings of the minds—living and otherwise. Mildly jealous of her more famous sister, as she aged, Isabella, who died at home in 1907 at the age of eighty-six, came to rely more on the advice of persons past than present. She insisted that the ghost of her dead mother, Harriet Porter Beecher, guided her in decisions from what speech to prepare to what dress to wear.

At one New Year's Eve gathering, Isabella alternately entertained the Clemenses—Olivia and Samuel, better known by his pen name, Mark Twain—and other neighbors and three mediums, whom she moved to upstairs bedrooms in a kind of human shell game. The evening ended after one of the mediums, a female of small build, ran down the stairs and beat up John Hooker—as she channeled the energy of an Indian warrior, she later explained.

We're Not as Snooty as All That

Hartford

Think Connecticut, and think stiff-upper-lip, tea at four, and the proper madras plaid shorts, right?

Well, sure, we're that and more. We are also a two-headed calf at one of Hartford's premier tourist stops, the Old State House. Upstairs in the 1796 Federal-style brick structure is a pretty accurate replica of John Steward's Museum of Curiosities.

A painter of some renown, Steward established a studio in the State House not long after it opened. Because painters were a dime a dozen, Steward began displaying curiosities among his artwork. He soon found that curiosities in an entertainment-starved culture were more profitable, so items like a stuffed two-headed calf, a unicorn horn, and shoes from the god Bacchus began to overtake his canvases and silhouettes.

Over the years, the collection was moved and pieces slipped away. No one knows what happened to the original two-headed calf, but in 1996 then-Executive Director Wilson H. Faude—himself no stranger to oddities—put out a call for another calf, and sure enough, he found one in Michigan. (The dual-headed calf is joined by, among other stuffed and preserved oddities, a two-headed piglet.)

Something you should know about Faude: He dressed like a preppie, but he was better at hucksterism than the state's own P. T. Barnum—if for no other reason than the so-called "window tax." To raise money for the Old State House at 800 Main Street, Faude declared that every business with a window overlooking the property should pay $10 per pane. He raised oodles of money that way and saved the landmark from the wrecking ball. While visiting, enjoy the Senate chamber, and the Supreme Courtroom, the site of famous trials such as the *Amistad* and Prudence Crandall cases. Call (860) 522–6766 for more information, or visit www.ctosh.org.

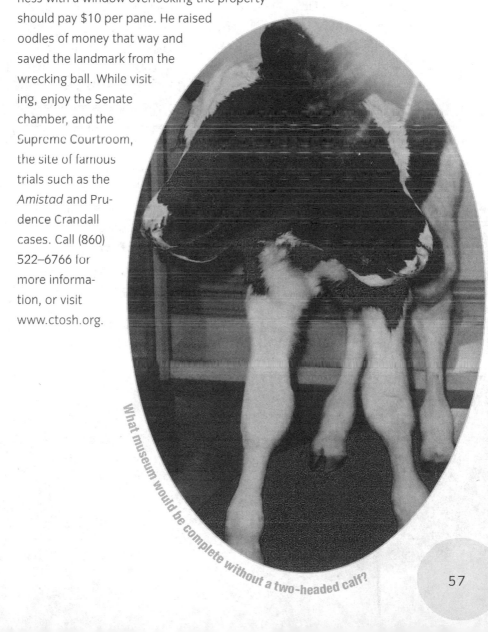

What museum would be complete without a two-headed calf?

Art as Rock
Hartford

Is it a big pile of rocks? Or is it art? In Hartford, it's both.

In 1977, artist Carl Andre installed what he called *Stone Field Structure,* an arrangement of thirty-six large boulders ranging from 1,000 pounds to ten tons and placed in a triangular pattern on a small strip of grass along Gold Street between Main and Lewis, near the historic Center Church.

At the time of its installation, *Structure* was called "minimalist sculpture," but most wags just called it a pile of rocks. The ensuing controversy was known as the "Great Art Debate of '77." The mayor at the time, George Athanson, gave the traditional modern art critique when he said, "Little kids could do that."

The city has slowly come to embrace the sculpture, which proved to be Andre's only outdoor commission. Rocks or art? Decide for yourself on Gold Street.

Art rocks on.

The Day the Clowns Cried
Hartford

On July 6, 1944, a fire of mysterious origins raced quickly around Ringling Brothers & Barnum and Bailey's tent, which was soaked in gasoline and paraffin for waterproofing. The fast-moving fire trapped 6,000 fans inside. Some escaped only because they were shoved out of openings slit by a hundred pocket knives owned by a hundred little boys. Some were carried out.

Some didn't make it.

The official toll was 168 dead and 682 injured, and the scene was so horrific that some victims could be identified only by the jewelry they wore. One infant was burned so badly that its remains were disposed of at the hospital. The State Armory on Broad Street became a morgue. All the bodies were claimed save for six, which were buried at Northwood Cemetery. One, who was known for years as Little Miss 1565 (the morgue number), was a little girl who'd been trampled, not burned, to death. Her identity remained a mystery until years later, when a Hartford arson investigator was able to identify her as Eleanor Cook, age eight, who'd gone to the circus that day with her mother and two brothers. One brother died from his injuries the next day. In 1991, Eleanor Cook's body was exhumed and buried in Massachusetts, next to her brother.

The fire's cause is still not known. What is known is that it was the worst circus fire in the country's history. In 2005, the Hartford Circus Fire Memorial was dedicated behind Fred D. Wish Elementary School at 350 Barbour.

The Only Monument to Hunger Strikers, Ever
Hartford

Organizers who helped raise money for a large Celtic cross dedicated to Bobby (Robert George) Sands and others who starved themselves to death while seeking to be recognized as political prisoners say there's no other memorial like it anywhere. And they're probably right.

The Maple Avenue traffic circle in Hartford's south end, on which the cross now sits, was dedicated to Sands and others in 1995. Two years later, the cross was added. Sands, the leader and perhaps the best known of the group of ten men, had served four years in a prison in Belfast, Northern Ireland, for weapons possession and membership in the Irish Republican Army before he began a hunger strike in March 1981. Nine other inmates joined the protest, at staggered times because, as Sands reasoned, stretching out the strike would focus the world's attention on their plight longer. During the strike, Sands was elected as a Member of Parliament for Fermanagh and South Tyrone. He also wrote poetry and kept a journal. He died after sixty-six days on his hunger strike.

In fact, none of the hunger strikers survived. The last died in August 1981, and all their names are carved on the cross.

The Hartford chapter of the Irish Northern Aid Committee, which supports Irish republican causes, raised more than $15,000 for the memorial.

BOBBY SANDS 1981 ciocFaiòh ár la

This monument may be one of a kind for this country.

How to Stay Close to Your Work

Hartford

Anxious to commemorate the Civil War and the 400 Hartford soldiers who didn't return from battle, residents of the city of Hartford began to haggle over an appropriately solemn design.

The city finally agreed to construct a memorial arch—and not an obelisk, as did so many other towns—over the Ford Street bridge. That bridge once spanned the Park River, which flowed through Bushnell Park. The Park River was eventually buried, but the huge arch remains. Interred within the arch are the ashes of George Keller, who designed the structure, and his wife. Seems Keller loved his work so much that he hated to leave it. Others seem strangely drawn to the arch, as well. Six times in two years recently, some poor driver has driven into the structure.

Today visitors can walk up the ninety-six steps of the Soldier's and Sailor's Memorial Arch to get a good view of the park.

An arch with a view.

AMERICA'S OLDEST CONTINUOUSLY PUBLISHED NEWSPAPER

The *Hartford Courant,* which began publication in October 1764, has seen 'em come and seen 'em go.

In 1776 the newspaper, like other New England publications of the time, printed the "Declaration of Independence"—on page 4. Back then, news judgment was not a consideration. News was printed as it was received—and often, "news" was little more than reprints of letters or tavern gossip.

In 1806 the newspaper was indicted for criminal libel against the administration of Thomas Jefferson. It's been an interesting history. For more information, call (860) 241–6200, or visit www.courant.com.

Death with Class

Hartford

If you've got to go, you might as well go in style. Of the state's roughly 2,400 cemeteries, Cedar Hill Cemetery, at 453 Fairfield Avenue in Hartford's South End, is known for attracting the state's well-to-do. Katharine Hepburn is buried there in a simple grave nearly obscured by an overgrown bush.

Other notable dead include John Pierpont Morgan, the Alan Greenspan of his day; Wallace Stevens, a contemporary of Mark Twain who combined the unlikely careers of insurance executive and poet; Isabella Beecher Hooker, Harriet Beecher Stowe's sister and a notable early suffragist, and Horace Wells, who is credited with discovering nitrous oxide, or "laughing gas."

Sadly, Wells may have found his place at Cedar Hill early. Legend has it that he investigated his discovery a little too vigorously. He was jailed in New York while under the influence (and slashing prostitutes), and he

Here lies Horace Wells, whom we can thank for laughing gas.

hanged himself there in 1848. His gravestone features a relief that reads THERE SHALL BE NO PAIN.

Sad you're not a part of the throng? The people in the cemetery's office say not to worry. The cemetery has room for another hundred years' worth of notable departed.

Walking tours of the cemetery are available by calling (860) 956–3311, or visit the Web site at www.cedarhillcemetery.org.

Witches? We've Got Witches

Hartford

Salem, Massachusetts, may get the tourists, but Connecticut had its own witch scare before the folks to the north had even dreamed up familiars—or the dunking test.

In 1647, Alyse (or Achsah) Young was hanged at the site of the Old State House on Main Street in Hartford. Another woman, Lydia Gilbert, was tried as a witch in 1653. She was accused of using witchcraft to influence one man to shoot another. The man who shot the gun was fined twenty pounds. Like Alyse Young, Gilbert was hanged.

Others—all women—were tried and hanged as witches. (Despite the common belief, persons convicted of witchcraft were rarely burned in America. They were more often hanged, drowned, or crushed under large rocks—a manner of death that went by the more genteel name of "pressing," as one would a pair of pants.)

Legend is that a portion of Trinity College in Hartford's South End, known as "Gallows Hill," was also once the site of a witch hanging. The same legend holds for Hartford's South Green, located at the juncture of Main and Wethersfield. A Trinity College dance instructor, Judy Dworin, has written and performed a piece about the Connecticut witch trials, called "Burning."

A Piece of the True Tree

Hartford and Elsewhere

More rare than relics from the True Cross are pieces of Connecticut's beloved Charter Oak, but for years things like earrings and tie tacks said to have come from the fabled tree sold like hotcakes.

The Charter Oak figures prominently in Connecticut's history. In 1639 colonists wrote *The Fundamental Orders*, said to be the first written constitution that created a government. In 1662 the colonists negotiated a charter that gave them considerable freedom under Charles II. Over time, Britain did not look kindly upon this document, and in 1687 the British governor called a meeting at which he demanded to see the charter.

The charter was produced, but during the evening meeting, the candles were suddenly extinguished and the charter disappeared—hidden by Captain Joseph Wadsworth in a nearby great oak that before its death by storm in 1856 grew to be 30 feet in diameter.

This grandchild of the original Charter Oak has its own plaque.

That's a big tree, but over the years, purported relics proliferated at an astonishing rate. As Mark Twain said in 1868, there were enough relics from the Charter Oak to "build a plank road from here to Salt Lake City." A grandchild tree of the original Charter Oak grows at the corner of Gold and Main Streets, near the historic Center Church.

And as for the relics, today the Connecticut Historical Society has some authentic pieces made from the original oak, and the wife of an industrialist bound two biographies of her dead husband in the wood. As for all the others? Fuggedabout it!

An Onion Grows in Hartford

Hartford

Samuel Colt was one of America's early industrialists. He was also a big blowhard. In 1835 Colt patented the revolving-breech pistol and opened a new factory to manufacture pistols. That venture failed within six years. In 1847 he opened another brownstone factory in Hartford, which he topped with a Russian-influenced blue dome.

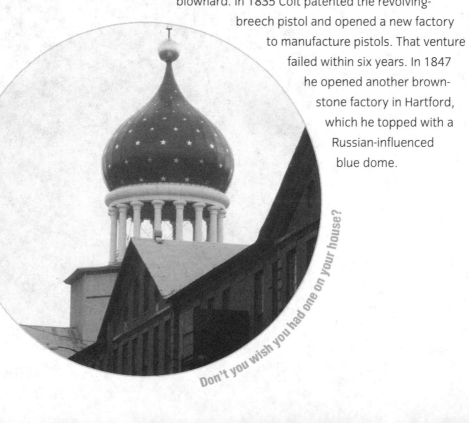

Don't you wish you had one on your house?

Around it, the aggressively self-aggrandizing Colt built what he thought would be a remarkable utopian factory complex that included worker housing and recreational areas. His wife, Elizabeth, organized day care centers. They christened it Coltsville, and historians say it turned Hartford into the "Silicon Valley of the nineteenth century."

But the high-living Samuel died in 1862 and left his wife to keep the business going. She did so assiduously, even through a disastrous 1864 fire that killed one employee and did $33 million in damage—and destroyed the beloved globe. Within two years the factory was rebuilt—this time in brick—and the blue, star-spangled globe, modeled after a church in Moscow, was replaced. The building itself is now under renovation.

Garage Door Magic
Manchester

We know there's a question that's been driving you crazy: Who had the first automatic garage door opener, anyway?

Why, it was a fire station in Manchester, sometime around the turn of the twentieth century. Whether it was the very first of its kind it's hard to say for certain, but one thing is clear: It was an amazing accomplishment. It was tied into the fire-alert system, and when the alarm for the station went off, an elaborate system of gears, weights, and pulleys opened the huge doors of the firehouse. The horses, kept behind the fire wagons, were so well trained that when they heard the bells and the doors, they knew to stop what they were doing and move to the front of their wagons to go to work.

If you find this interesting, we've barely scratched the surface of the unusual treasures that await you at the Fire Museum in Manchester (860–649–9436, www.thefiremuseum.org), which is the work of the

Connecticut Fireman's Historical Society. Located in the very firehouse that had those cool automatic doors (and served from 1901 until well into the 1960s), the museum now houses an amazing collection of fire-fighting equipment, hardware, and memorabilia, the scope of which you have to see to believe. A favorite is a Cataract, or New York–style pumper wagon from Meriden that dates back to 1851. This huge, hand-primed squirting device was used not only on fires but also on rival fire companies.

"It often put more water on firemen than it did on fires," laughs Dick Symonds, chairman of the Board of Trustees who helped make this fantastic museum a reality.

From a collection of sprinkler heads to cases filled with fire badges to scaling ladders and entire antique fire engines, this place has something guaranteed to surprise just about any firefighter, fire buff, or antiques aficionado.

Have Some Burger with Your Cheese
Manchester

Eateries that try to capture the charm of the '50s dairy bar/burger joint aren't exactly unusual. But what is truly odd is 1) a place that pulls off the retro ambience so well it actually made us feel we were locked in an endless loop of *American Graffiti*, and 2) an establishment that truly gives the term "cheeseburger" the righteous relevance it deserves. The Shady Glen Dairy Store at 840 Middle Turnpike East in Manchester (860–649–4245) is not a place one enters lightly. There are cow products in startling abundance, and a cheeseburger that is unique in the annals of Burgerdom.

Indeed, to order up Bernice's Large Cheeseburger is to secure a beef-pattied sandwich that is not just covered with cheese; the cheddar avenger jumped the patty in the alley, wrestled it to the ground and completely dominated it. Named for creator Bernice Reig, who it is said devised the world's first lactic attack comestible over three decades ago, the cheese on this rig overhangs to the point where the heat of the grill curves it up around the bun so it appears as if a clam is sticking its tongue out at you. When you first see the burg, as a period-dressed wait person (a lovely pine-green dress for the ladies, a white button-down with bow tie for the gents) gracefully sets it before you, the thought enters your mind that something in the grill area has gone horribly wrong. Clearly, the new guy had some trouble during the apply-the-cheese-to-the-burger phase of meal preparation.

But fear not. This is a cheeseburger the way the Great Cow intended, for it is quite possible that the bovine milk and flesh content on this unit are roughly equal. This means there is harmony, and that this could be the best-balanced burger in the known universe.

Bernice's special is what a balanced bovine sandwich is all about.

Naturally, one must complement this treat with fries and slaw, and one of the Glen's awesome milkshakes. For dessert their dairy roots are evident in the huge variety of ice cream available, which you can also purchase by the gallon. Everything is wholesome, tasty goodness, but the burger really is something special. Thanks, Bernice.

Jukebox in the Round
Manchester

It's a sad day, indeed, and a conundrum of significant proportions, when your jukes aren't juking properly. You want to hang out and lean against your trusty Wurlitzer like a modern-day James Dean, but you can't get the box to play your tunes. You need a new jukebox, or you'd like to get a classic model restored to its former glory. What do you do?

From jukes to classic 45s, this shop is a gold mine of retro treasures.

Better yet, who ya gonna call?

You call (or better yet, visit) New England Jukebox and Amusement Company in Manchester (860–646–1533). For nearly two decades, Steve Hanson's company has been collecting, restoring, and selling jukeboxes, pinball machines, foosball tables, and countless other machines and memorabilia. They also sell brand-new jukeboxes, such as the Wurlitzer 1015, a replica of their 1946 model.

But it's the restored models that are the most intriguing, and employee Scott Duncan says that if an old jukebox shows up with all its pieces, they can probably get it running: "As long as they're complete and they're standing, they will get restored," he says with a smile.

The store is literally filled with treasures. A Seeburg circular jukebox watches from the corner, like a huge, silent R2–D2 from *Star Wars*. There are plenty of old 45s and record collections, as diverse as Bing Crosby classics to "The Red Army Sings." A huge collection of old radios resides on one wall, while a classic Schwinn Sting Ray "Pea Picker" hangs from the ceiling. But it's jukeboxes that rule the roost here, and it's a great place to bring youngsters who have no idea how "Twist and Shout" was first delivered to teenagers.

"I've got kids coming in here all the time who have never even seen a jukebox," explains Hanson.

The Evolution of the Toaster
New Britain

How many times have you seen the famous Darwinian illustration in which, in subsequent drawings, we see how man might have evolved from ape into hockey player over the centuries? Have you ever wondered how toasters evolved? Or egg beaters? Or even ball bearings?

The New Britain Industrial Museum located on the Central Connecticut State University campus in New Britain (860–832–8654; www.nbim.org) illustrates such amazing mechanical evolution by displaying the actual products themselves. How can they do this? Simple. The New Britain area was once a hotbed of some of the most innovative (and now commonplace) products ever created by man—or hockey player. In fact, it used to be called the Hardware Center of the World.

"There was really no reason for this area to become one of the most important industrial centers in the country, other than the incredible talent of its people," explains the museum's Warren Kingsbury. "There was no river here to drive machinery, so like everything else they needed, they built their own reservoirs to power the plants. These were incredibly inventive people."

A stroll through this place will leave you amazed. From the North and Judd Company's famous horse tack (and its relation to Buffalo Bill) to the creation of the first electric coffeepot, the history of so many products we take for granted is here, in items you can actually touch and examine. And the collection of electric toasters, from items that basically were dangerous yeast-frying firetraps to the slick devices we're used to now, is not to be missed.

These toasters could turn bread into kindling in a New York second.

Pop with Class

New Britain

It's tough to find a soft drink company that doesn't have a major star or two hawking their product on television. It's even harder to find one that makes flavors that a true soda connoisseur can appreciate—tasty concoctions that go beyond the mundane flavors we've allowed to dominate the marketplace.

But Avery's in New Britain (860–340–0830, www.averysoda.com) can take care of your carbonated beverage needs, for they truly hand-craft every bottle of liquid joy they sell. The Avery name has been on soda pop since 1904, and the company still does things in a low-volume way that ensures the kind of quality you can't get from the big soda conglomerates.

"We view our soda as kind of a gourmet product, sort of a micro-brewed soda pop," says owner Rob Metz. "We have low volume, which means we can tightly control the quality. We use the best ingredients, like pure cane sugar instead of coarse sugar like you get at the supermarket."

There's some serious soda inside this bottle.

Like variety? Avery's has about thirty standard flavors and a special-edition Flavor of the Month. You can actually watch such exotics as Watermelon or Kiwi get bottled, too, as the machinery is right there in the store. Even the bottles are cool, and you can't beat the taste.

"It's a great place to come and show kids how things used to be done," says Metz. Big kids will love it, too.

Two Whole Feet of Pink Goodness

Newington

You walk in the door and see a cozy, retro, one-room sort of establishment that promises real-deal burgers and fries. There's '50s decor, and the delicious smell of fried onions on the grill that lures you over for a closer look.

It was clear upon arrival: Either bypass the two-foot hot dog or get a longer motorcycle.

Then you see them—sitting on the grill like so many plump, pink eels. These are no mere hot dogs; oh, no. These are Doogie's Two-Foot-Long Hot Dogs, and they make normal hot dogs look like mere cocktail wienies by comparison. These are the dogs that try men's souls—or at least their stomach capacities.

But wait. You say you have no hankering for 24-plus inches of pink goodness? These titanic tubular taste treats are only one item on a menu of excellent fare, including (grilled, not fried, dammit) burgers with the usual toppings—and then some. There's a certain old-fashioned quality to this eatery located in Newington on the Berlin Turnpike (860–666–6200), and that goes right down to the principles of the place, which are clearly posted on the wall for all to see. These include:

"We're neither slow nor fast. We're half fast. Great food takes time."

"If you're cranky—come back another day."

"If you don't like the way I run my business, buy me out."

You've got to love a place that has the courage to make their dogs curiously long, and put their principles on the wall for the world to see.

Built like a Concrete Whale

West Hartford

You see it, and you can't help but think of Jonah and the whale. Or maybe you'll fancy yourself a color-blind Captain Ahab. Regardless, Conny the sperm whale, outside the Children's Museum in West Hartford (860–231–2830, www.thechildrensmuseumct.org), is a striking sight. Here we have a beached whale with no tragic loss of life, for Conny is made of concrete and is a full-size replica of a seagoing mammal, complete with a blowhole that does its stuff about every four minutes (in warm weather). A doorway carved in the side lets you see what it's like from the standpoint of a giant squid (a sperm whale's favorite entree), making this perhaps the only walk-in sperm whale in existence.

Another unique walk-in at this center is the world's largest kaleidoscope—a huge, walk-in version of the visually vexing creations that consist of a tube you rotate to observe glorious geometric patterns. If you still haven't satisfied your craving for big things, there's also a 45-foot-long Foucalt pendulum, an enormous plum bob that allows you to actually observe the rotation of the earth over time. All these science-based attractions are designed to stimulate kids and adults alike, and the eclectic selection of exhibits (from a Turtle Town with live reptile residents to a small studio that lets you play TV meteorologist) makes this a very unusual and rewarding place to play.

Throw your harpoon in this, matey, and you'll need a new harpoon.

THE SOUTHWICK JOG

Along Connecticut's northern boundary there is a hitch known as the Southwick Jog—a 6-square-mile piece of Massachusetts that juts into Connecticut along what is otherwise a fairly straight border.

The line was originally drawn in 1642 by Nathaniel Woodward and Solomon Saffrey, two men known for their professionalism and artistry—but who had trouble drawing a straight line. They started southwest of Boston, sailed around Cape Cod, into Long Island Sound, and up the Connecticut River to set their next marker. They were a little south of where they needed to be, and that area—what is now Enfield—was disputed for decades.

You could say that Connecticut won that dispute but lost Southwick. It was said for years that the notch served as a tab, keeping Massachusetts from sliding into the sea. Others say Woodward and Saffrey were frightened by Algonquin Indians as they tried to draw their straight line—or maybe they were tippling, just a bit. Either way, the notch and its Congamond Lakes, which provided power for mills in the area, remain Massachusetts land.

By 1820 Connecticut had conceded the land, although state officials have issued subsequent threats to overtake it. They're kidding, of course. A volunteer organization, Citizens Restoring Congamond, keeps the place looking splendiferous. While there, try the fare at Crabby Joe's.

Where Doody Reigns
West Hartford

He's a rather wooden character, but he has a smile that's contagious, and his easygoing western demeanor is considered charming and downright charismatic by young people. Are we talking about a new young star of the big screen?

Nah, this guy's a lot older than most teen idols. We're talking about Howdy Doody, who ruled the TV world in the '50s. And in his American Dream Museum in West Hartford (860–561–5311, www.neilsdream .com), Neil Sakow has amassed the most incredible collection of Howdy Doody memorabilia anywhere. Howdy had his lovable mug on everything from sneakers to drapes, and Neil has been collecting representatives of just about every item with the tiny star's visage since he was six. His father had a shop that sold such cool merchandise, which naturally facilitated the process.

Incidentally, Howdy was only the beginning. Neil has not created just a shrine for a famous TV personality but a rather terrific museum with three floors of all kinds of memorabilia from the '50s and '60s, including special collections of Mickey Mantle and JFK artifacts.

I Love Lucy fans will find some pretty amazing finds, such as Desi Arnaz's conga drums, and Neil even has a collection of wedding photos from when Lucille and Desi tied the knot. To add to the intrigue of this huge collection, Neil even has boxes and boxes of artifacts that even he hasn't opened since they were put away new, and their exact contents are a mystery that he plans on revealing when the time is right. This is a unique museum run by a great guy, and you should definitely check it out.

A House Full of Words

West Hartford

Who among us at some point in their personal history hasn't either perused, studied, thrown, or used for its sheer heftiness (such as a doorstop or gravity clamp when gluing some broken objet d'art) a *Webster's Dictionary*?

I think we have all met up with this formidable volume, but have you ever wondered what kind of mind it would take to tediously record all the words in a given language? We have, and it boggles our minds, to say the least. Here in Connecticut we have the unusual opportunity to gain some insight into the upbringing of Noah Webster, the man who brought the first American dictionary to the world.

The Noah Webster House Museum of West Hartford History (860–521–5362, www.noahwebsterhouse.org) is a beautifully restored peek back into New England history courtesy of the amazing scribe's childhood home. Noah lived here the first sixteen years of his life before heading off to Yale, and thanks to guides dressed in period costume and a variety of artifacts from the era, you can get a glimpse into the life of his Connecticut family and maybe, just maybe, get some clues as to how he became so patient, well organized, and scholarly. You'll find out that after college Noah became a teacher and became so disgusted that there were so few genuine American textbooks, he started his literary legacy by writing a grammar book that became known as the *Blue Back Speller*. He eventually moved on to the dictionary, and the rest is reference history.

The house is the place, we're convinced, where the words that Noah would later put down on paper first started swirling around in his head. Inhale the ambience, and see if you can detect the faintest whiff of "pernicious," "discombobulated," or any other wild terms that may well

Noah Webster's childhood home was clearly a place of great in-house Scrabble games.

have been subtly working their way into the young Webster's psyche.
There are some period activities you can engage in, and with a visit to
this fine home you gain an appreciation for the life the Webster family
and countless other New Englanders experienced on a daily basis.

Sumatra in Connecticut

Windsor

You may think you know a thing or two about Connecticut, but do you know about the Havana connection?

Actually, there is no Havana connection that we know of. But there *is* a Dominican Republic connection, a Nicaraguan connection, and connections with countless other Latin American countries because of the extraordinary quality of Connecticut Shade tobacco.

Confused? Are you thinking that we've left Connecticut for the massive tobacco barns of Kentucky? Has this become *Kentucky Kuriosities*?

Nah, we've just been to the Luddy/Taylor Connecticut Valley Tobacco Museum in Windsor (860–285–1888, www.tobaccohistsoc.org). There's no better place to learn about the history of the very special tobacco grown here, which is used to wrap the world's finest cigars. If you've ever flown into Bradley International Airport, you've no doubt seen strange white "tents" in fields around the airfield. Instead of small suburban circus companies or Bedouin campsites, you are viewing enclosed areas re-creating the humid growing environment of Sumatra, where the fine tobacco strains used today originally came from. This used to be an enormous business in Connecticut, as the museum's delightful curator, Marion Nielson, attests:

"In the old days there were more than 30,000 acres of tobacco being farmed; now there are only about 2,000," she explains. "But the tobacco grown here is used in some of the finest cigars in the world, and there's still money to be made."

The museum displays a great assortment of specialized equipment that's been used over the years, as well as all kinds of documentation on how Connecticut Shade tobacco (and its less fancy kin, the Broadleaf) became an international sensation.

Voices from Above

Windsor Locks

It was a strange sensation, and for a moment there we started to question our sanity. Not that doing such a thing is unusual for us, you understand; it's just that when the voices in your head start to echo throughout the room, you get uneasy.

It happened as we were gazing at an old Douglas DC–3 passenger plane in the Civil Aircraft Hangar of the New England Air Museum, Windsor Locks (860–623–3305, www.neam.org). We distinctly heard the voice of an American Airlines pilot talking to an air traffic controller,

Is it a plane or a boat?

and subsequent investigation revealed we were not alone in hearing these disembodied voices. Other visitors were hearing them, too, and it turns out that the pilots were actually real people and not just auditory phantoms. To add some atmosphere to the exhibit area, the museum was broadcasting a radio feed from the FAA next door at Bradley International Airport. It was quite effective.

As interesting as the audio is, though, it's the visual treasures that make this museum special. Remember the era of the Flying Boat? This museum has one of only a few survivors of the breed, a perfectly restored Sikorsky VS–44A returned to its native Connecticut after serving all over the world. Want something stranger? How about a GeeBee R-1 Supersportster racer replica built by the museum with the stipulation that it would never fly? Because the wildly designed (it looks like all engine and very little plane) R–1 was such a handful at speed, it even made legendary pilot Jimmy Doolittle nervous. The original manufacturer wouldn't hand over the blueprints for the project unless the museum promised not to fly it. Yikes!

Inside and out, you'll find amazing, unique flying objects in a wonderfully well-organized setting. Don't forget to wander around outside, where you'll find that Chinese-built Soviet MiG–15 fighter you've been searching for all your life.

NORTHEAST

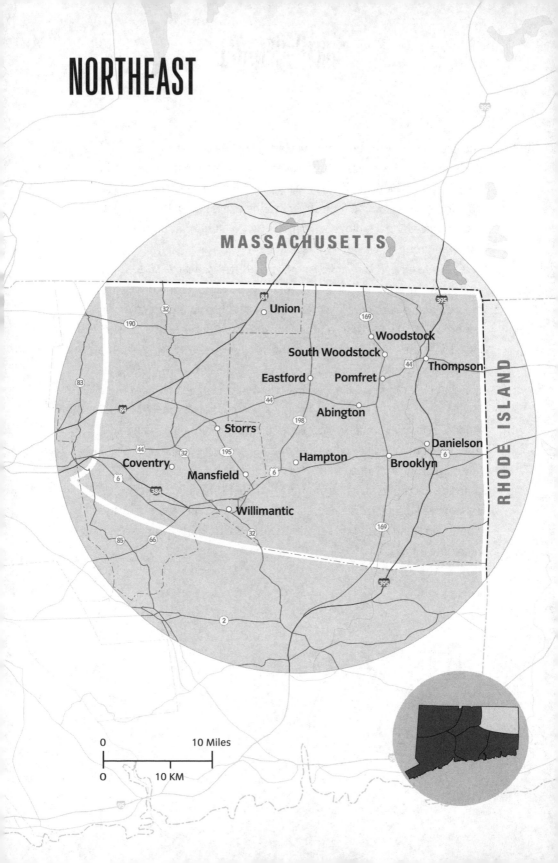

MASSACHUSETTS

RHODE ISLAND

Union

Woodstock

South Woodstock

Eastford   Pomfret   Thompson

Abington

Storrs

Coventry   Hampton   Danielson

Mansfield   Brooklyn

Willimantic

0   10 Miles

0   10 KM

NORTHEAST

Lost in the Ice Cream Rush

Abington

Certain things just seem to go together, don't you think? One day an enterprising cook slapped a slab of cheddar cheese on a patty of ground meat and presto! The cheeseburger was born. In some circles, folks see the two food items that make up a cheeseburger to be inseparable.

And some other individuals (well, OK, us) now consider incredibly rich homemade ice cream to be inseparable from corn mazes. By the way, when we say "maze" we don't mean maize, which is obviously spelled differently and is a type of corn. The maze we're talking about is (as *Webster's* says) "a confusing, intricate network of pathways; labyrinth." This one is all-natural, too, for it is carved through a field of corn that's growing as high as an elephant's eye.

Walking this labyrinth after eating ice cream is a truly spiritual experience.

Here's the deal: The We-Li-Kit farm has been serving fantastic home-made ice cream to northeast Connecticut for many years from their modest stand located on Route 97 in Abington (860–974–1095). But there's a problem: So rich and fantastic are these desserts that the sugar rush leaves you needing to burn off some energy (and some calories). In response to these needs, the We-Li-Kit clan has on occasion constructed (when crop conditions allow) an excellent maze in their cornfield across the street from the ice-cream stand. It's a delightful green jungle that is a great place to get lost in for young and old alike. By the time you find your way out, you're usually sufficiently weakened that you may have to go back for seconds. How great is that?

Shuffling the Buffalo
Brooklyn

"Now that's something you don't see every day," we commented to a Rottweiler of our acquaintance, and he seemed to agree. This particular dog happens to be quite familiar with the livestock in this area, such as horses, cows, and the odd deer that wanders out of the forest.

But this creature was different, and the dog seemed a trifle confused. The beast we watched amble back and forth looked like either a small woolly mammoth or an unusually large poodle with horns. But it was actually a bison, or a buffalo, which is the bison's pen name.

Creamery Brook Bison Farm (860–779–0837, www.creamerybrook bison.com) on Purvis Road in Brooklyn has been raising buffalo and selling the meat to the public since 1990. They tout the meat's health benefits compared with beef and sell a lot of the lean stuff to discerning types who want something other than a conventional hamburger. The farm also gives tours so that you can see these wily beasts in action.

A full-grown bison weighs a ton, can run 35 mph and can jump a 6-foot fence. This makes them a bit feistier than your average Holstein—except for Thunderbolt, of course. Thunderbolt is a six-year-old who was bottle-fed since birth and has a much nicer disposition. He's considered a pet, although we can't imagine that he's housebroken, and we'd hate to see him chase a cat through the house at top speed. Yikes!

LOOK, MA! NO MORTAR

Lining two-lane country roads and snaking across the horizon of distant hills in eastern Connecticut is a maze of rock walls, many of them built by colonists looking for a creative way to use the rocks they dug up as they plowed their fields.

The rocks—many of them now covered with lace-doily lichen that will eventually break down the rocks and destroy them—were simply stacked atop one another to make a wall. There is no mortar holding them together, but the farmers knew what they were doing. Some of the walls have stood for 200-plus years. Their biggest predator is the contractors who dismantle them to recreate the look of old New England in new housing developments—that, and the aforementioned lichen.

A particularly pretty assortment of rock walls lines fields along Route 169 at the northern border of Canterbury.

The Ghost and Mr. Cook

Coventry

A day before she died in December 1997, ninety-three-year-old Adelma Grenier Simmons drew up a deathbed will for her internationally famous, fifty-acre herb farm, Caprilands. Her division of her worldly goods was not precisely what some family members expected—the farm was left to a nonprofit foundation.

During her life, Ms. Simmons, "the grande dame of American herbalists," offered entertaining lectures and lunches. For a half century she ruled over her lamb's ear and parsnip, her tansy and Scotch broom, with a lovingly imperial hand. For those who knew her, it was hard to imagine the grande dame as anything but in complete control.

Today Caprilands (860–742–7244) still attracts people from all over New England, but there is a difference. These days Ms. Simmons is supposed to inhabit the place—as a ghost. A few longtime customers have sworn that they've seen a figure resembling the elderly woman on the property. Or they've heard her in the tearoom.

Look for her at Caprilands on Silver Street; take Route 44 to 534 Silver.

The Horse as Pharaoh

Coventry

It's weird how certain geographic shapes can attract you—even hold some sort of strange meaning in your psyche that you don't quite understand. At the Nathan Hale Homestead in Coventry (860–742–6917, http://ursamajor.hartnet.org/als/nathanhale/) a strange conical structure behind the main house gives the passerby an eerie feeling, as though the former home of the famous patriot ("I regret that I have but one life to lose for my country") is also the resting place of a Colonial pharaoh.

The structure is a pyramid, or more precisely a rock cairn, with strange writing at its base. Hieroglyphics, perhaps? Could this be a cheaper version of the alien obelisk in the old *Star Trek* episode where Captain Kirk lost his memory? Nah, it's just Latin. And the cairn does not mark the burying place of a member of the Hale family, but a horse.

"It was put there by the gentleman who restored the house, George Dudley Seymour, in an early part of the twentieth century," explains the Homestead's Desiree Mobed. "He had a much loved horse, Thomas Hooker Bones, that lived nearly forty years. When the horse died, he decided to build him a fitting monument."

The inscription, which briefly chronicles Bones' life from the Spanish-American War to time he spent in Hartford, says, "He was a noble breed, and may the earth rest lightly on him."

That may be difficult under all those rocks, but the pyramid is a lovely structure for what was apparently a very special animal.

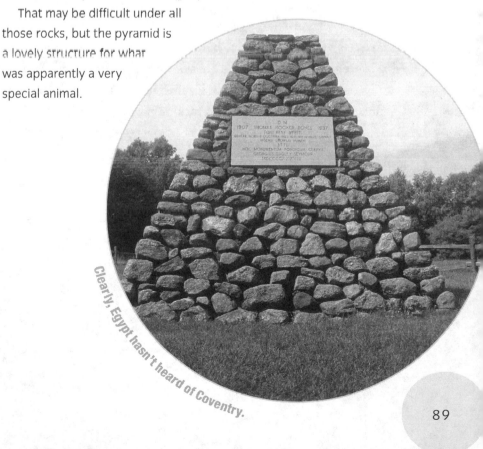

Clearly, Egypt hasn't heard of Coventry.

FROM RAILS TO TRAILS

The quickest path between two points is a straight line, right?

You bet. And so railroad engineers and others decided the fastest way from Boston to New York would look like someone had drawn a line through the air.

The Air Line was born, the brainchild of the New York and Boston Railroad Company.

Ah, if only life were so simple. The company was tied up in court while competing companies and Hartford business people, afraid they were about to lose a sizeable chunk of their passenger business, tried everything to block the company's dream. Tying up those legal loose ends took a considerable amount of time, and then there was the Connecticut River to bridge, a small matter of a funding scandal, and fairly large rock ridges to cut through.

There's more to the story—there's always more to the story—but suffice it to say that the project was completed in the 1870s, some twenty years later than was expected, and was countless dollars over budget. No matter. In the 1880s, train cars painted white with gold trim, and run by porters dressed all in white, ferried delighted passengers back and forth. For people without a ticket, the train came to be known as the Ghost Train.

Like all good things, the Ghost Train came to an end, and the last passenger train used the Air Line railway in 1902. Except for a few small sections, freight trains stopped using the railway in the 1960s.

Today, part of the former rail bed is a roughly 50-mile-long hiking trail that stretches from the Massachusetts border to the Connecticut River. In the Colchester and East Hampton area, the trail runs over two viaducts that offer panoramic views in all direction. Years ago, a small depot sat at the Lyman Viaduct.

If the railway didn't work for trains, it works great for hikers, bikers, and anyone else propelling themselves on their own steam. Local parks and recreation departments sponsor an annual run in the fall. The trail is constantly being improved, and it's considered one of the best greenways in the state. For directions to the closest portion of the trail to you, visit http://pages .cthome.net/mbartel/ARRabout.htm.

The Kitty Vanishes
Coventry

Some things in life endure. No matter what may happen to the world around these institutions, they continue to stay with us.

Of course, if the institution in question happens to be a gravesite for a cat, then the thing is liable to up and disappear on you. This is what patrons of the Bidwell Tavern in Coventry (860–742–6978) discovered, when this local watering hole (which has been around in various forms since 1712) recently changed owners.

The story goes that at a previous change of ownership, the new owners were told that in addition to the tavern itself (and a colorful history that dates back to the days of Nathan Hale), they were also taking charge of a cat that had lived at the tavern for years. The friendly feline was a permanent fixture, and there was even a photo near the bar of the Bidwell's "mascot" wearing a Santa Claus hat and drinking milk out of a shot glass.

A hotbed of feline mystery and intrigue.

Unfortunately, after a long and glorious reign as the official tavern cat, the affable kitty passed on. In honor of this singular animal, a gravesite with a rather classy tombstone was erected outside the building. This became a Bidwell landmark, as recognizable as the old timber frames in the bar itself, which date back to the original tavern.

Then it happened. Shortly after the latest change in ownership, the grave marker (and perhaps the grave itself) and photo of the beloved cat vanished. No one seems to know what happened, although the prevailing theory is that someone attached to the cat (possibly the previous owners) moved the final resting place to their home. Bidwell soldiers on, though, and continues to be one of Coventry's favorite gathering places.

A Lemon Grows in Connecticut

Danielson

Straight back from Logee's Greenhouses retail shop, with a little jog to the right, there grows a giant, 101-year-old lemon tree—*Citrus limon*—where the fruits are softball-sized and the scent hits you long before you even see it.

That's not all. There are begonias, jasmine—anything you could find in a rain forest—in this maze of a northeast Connecticut greenhouse. Not only are these rare finds in the northeast, the flowers, buds, and fruit are usually three and four times as big as anything you'll see anywhere else in the country.

Logee's (LOG-e's) was started in 1892 by plant lover William David Logee on a site he rented from a local cobbler. He fathered fifteen children, all of whom worked in the greenhouse and one of whom—Ernest, the eldest—rebuilt the greenhouse at age twenty-one. It was Ernest who started cultivating begonias, and now Logee's is known worldwide for its collection.

Sister Joy started a mail-order business, and the greenhouses' plants grew to include 2,500 varieties. They don't do anything small at Logee's. Walking through the maze of greenhouses is like walking through a rain forest. In fact, many of the plants that do best in this environment are usually found *only* in southern climes. The dirt in the greenhouses is so fertile that a seed often accidentally drops and then rather quickly grows into a giant. Those little buds on the plants in your dining room hang bigger than an adult forearm at Logee's.

The business is in its third generation of ownership and is getting quite famous among plant lovers, and the greenhouses are showing up in all kinds of publications. See for yourself at Logee's Greenhouses on North Street in Danielson. Call (888) 330–8038, or visit them at www.logees.com.

State nicknames: Constitution State, Provision State (we supplied a lot of the stuff for the army in the Revolutionary War, and don't you forget it), Nutmeg State (not necessarily a good thing), and—keep this one to yourself because it's damn embarrassing—Land of Steady Habits.

Every Froggy Must Get Stoned
Eastford

Tooling fast on Route 44, you're liable to miss one of eastern Connecticut's mildly hidden roadside attractions—a piece of folk art that dots the roads out Eastford way. Slow down, though, as you near Pomfret heading east, and you might catch a glimpse of the famous Frog Rock, its color a little faded, its site blocked off by signs.

And maybe, as you look closely, you'll think it resembles not an amphibian but a flounder. Whatever. The rock ain't arguing, and perhaps we're just quibbling. The area was once a roadside picnic stop, but when Route 44 was renovated a few years ago, the site was blocked off. You can still see it—and walk to it—but you have to be paying attention.

The frog rock, tucked behind some brush, stands sentinel on Route 44.

The frog was the brainchild of Thomas Thurber, a Republican state legislator in the 1880s. He passed the rock many times on his way to the Capitol in Hartford and, one day in 1881, he painted the rock to look more like what he thought it looked like already—a frog poised to jump.

State legislators could do those kinds of things in those days. Since then the frog has faded a little, but in 1997 descendants of Thurber repainted it. The descendants restored it to its proper green—and painted a tribute to Thurber on an adjacent rock. They've promised to keep it maintained in perpetuity, so consider this a frog with an infinite future.

The Sweater That Screams

Hampton

Here in the wilds of northeastern Connecticut, we certainly have our share of critters. Wild turkeys roam in packs, occasionally chasing innocent children from bus stops and striking terror in the hearts of ticks and other small, edible insects. Foxes are seen on occasion, and then there are the odd bobcat and fisher sightings (the latter being a robust member of the otter family who emits a scream that would make Faye Wray proud). Deer are regular residents, as are horses, cows, opossums, and the occasional coyote. Oh, and then there's the other animal that screams like a woman being chased by a giant ape—the sweater-friendly herbivore known as the alpaca.

"Hold on now," you whine. "Aren't alpacas native to the Andes of Peru, and don't they stalk the mountains like mountain goats yet donate their wonderful fur to make some of the most amazingly warm and soft clothing on earth?"

Well, first of all, we are impressed with your knowledge of mammals and textiles. But there are also alpacas in Connecticut, roaming (in a fenced-in sort of way) happily about at the Safe Haven Alpaca Farm at 39 Drain Street in Hampton (860-455-0054, www.safehavenalpaca .com). This quirk of Connecticut ecology was made possible by Texas transplant Edie Roxburgh, and when she moved from Houston to Hampton several years ago she had no idea she would one day look out her window to see the same sort of creature as many a Peruvian farmer has roaming about on their property. What started as a spacious, quiet new home has grown into something quite unexpected, and wonderfully unique.

Alpacas may be native to Peru, but they're roaming the Hampton countryside, too.

"The house itself was four years in construction," Roxburgh explains, "and once I finally got into it I realized I had ninety acres and I'm a real energetic, go-getter kind of a lady. I thought, what can I do with this land?"

Amazingly, it was a simple magazine ad that said, "Alpacas: An investment you can hug," that got the ball rolling. Long story short, Roxburgh did extensive research on the woolly beasts and not only saw a great business opportunity but fell in love with the interesting creatures. She cleared land, built a barn, and now is not only breeding alpacas for sale (and their wool, which she sells in yarn form), but has expanded the business into other areas.

"Once I got the alpacas here I needed to show people what you do with them, and so I opened the retail store with the alpaca clothing," Roxburgh continues. "We changed this into a country store when my manager [Val Agostinelli] realized we needed local products our guests might be interested in, like local honey, syrups, jams, and jellies, and that kind of thing. This is how it all evolved."

So now she has a bed and breakfast where you can relax and hear the scream of the alpaca (rare, but unforgettable), and purchase alpaca clothing, local yummables, or a whole beast (some folks like a bit of Peru in their households). As for these relatives of the camel, you really need to come see how charming they are. Much shorter than their camel and llama relatives, these rascals climb, hum, and I'm told they spit (like camels), but only when appropriate. Like the alpacas, the house, farm, and family-run business are warm and friendly, and welcome visitors year round.

The Rigby "Cathedral"

Hampton

It's a building that looks so happy and comfortable in its surroundings, you'd assume it has always resided where it now stands. It hasn't.

The small, elegant structure is adorned with an absolutely stunning stained-glass window, so it clearly must be a house of worship of some sort. It isn't.

Well, that's not exactly true. We must remember that everything depends on one's perspective. One person's church is another person's restored railroad freight building that was moved across town and fitted with a stained glass window that was discovered at a thrift shop.

Confused? It's simple—sort of.

Three-for-one: a church, an artist's studio, and a railroad freight building.

If you head north on Main Street in Hampton and then take a left when you get to Kenyon Road, you have only to journey just past the lovely home at 72 Kenyon and look to your right to see an unusual structure. A tall A-frame building with a huge stained-glass window, the building started life as a freight building for the Hampton rail station a few miles away. It was moved to its present location adjoining a Hampton home many years ago, and when the Rigby family purchased the property in the early 1990s, it became the art studio for Paul Rigby, an award-winning political cartoonist and painter. One day while on an outing to Brooklyn, Connecticut, the family made an interesting discovery:

"We saw this stained-glass window leaning up against the barn in the back of the Rocking Horse Farm and decided to have a look at it," Paul recounts. "There were several windows and things from cathedrals and such, but this one was in the best shape. On the spot, we decided to buy it; it turned out to fit in perfectly when installed in the studio."

Local craftsman Lenny Patera, of the Hampton Remodeling Company (860–455–1340), tackled the job of gently coaxing an old church window (an incredibly heavy one at that, for it is composed largely of lead) into the old railroad freight building turned artist's studio. He did a magnificent job, and even though the Rigbys have moved south, the "cathedral" remains as a neat touch in a lovely neighborhood.

Celebrating the Diversity of the Tomato
Hampton

You really need to keep your eyes on folks after they retire, because a lot of the time their newfound free time results in some absolutely wonderful mischief.

Take Hampton's John Sokoloski. This pharmacologist from Yale retired to Hampton, and over the past four years has transformed from drug lord (the good kind, not a criminal) to tomato wizard. He has many other plants in his garden, but when you raise 180 different varieties of tomatoes, you're doing some serious horticulture.

"I wouldn't say I'm an expert on them, but I do have quite a few," laughs Sokoloski. "I became very interested in the genetic diversity of plants and how this has been diminished by the hybridization of genetically modified seeds and so forth. So when we moved here to Hampton, I started gardening and became really interested in tomatoes. They're fun to grow, and there are so many styles, shapes, and colors. I think they're really beautiful."

Sokoloski has done such an amazing job at cultivating so many types of rare tomatoes that he has become well known in food circles. He has even been featured on radio talk shows featuring fine dining. He also holds tastings in the summer where friends and neighbors are invited to sample some truly unusual tomatoes that are as delicious as they are un-tomato-like in appearance. Amazingly, though, Sokoloski wouldn't claim any deep knowledge about the taste side of his creations: "The irony is, I enjoy them in sauces," he says, "but I don't eat fresh tomatoes."

But Do They Get Mirrored Ceilings?
Hampton

It's not too unusual to see new technology pop up in industries like aerospace or coffee makers, but here in the ruggedly sedate Quiet Corner of Connecticut, technology boldly sets trends in areas that might just surprise you. Case in point: cows.

I'm not talking about just any cows, either. I'm referring to our wonderfully dedicated Connecticut dairy cows, who give other domestic and foreign dairy cows a real run for their money in productivity. The fact is, Connecticut is a tough place for running a dairy farm, due to many factors, not the least of which is our weather. But our farmers have learned to compete in a variety of ways, and the tricks of the trade revolve around one fundamental truth: A happy cow is a productive cow. The Woodhill Farm in Hampton is dedicated to cow comfort, and to this end was one of the first in this part of the country to introduce a technology that is actually pretty wild when you think about it: the waterbed.

Yeah, baby! If this barn's rocking, well, it just means all the cows are moving around at once. So why a waterbed, anyway? Are we saying that cows are happiest reliving the '80s, when waterbeds were all the rage?

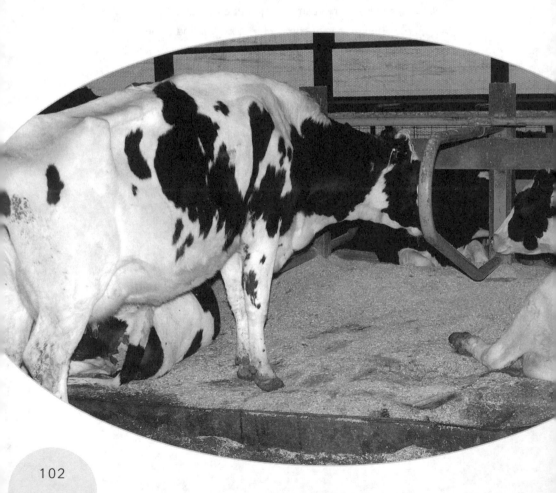

As usual the reason involves many factors, as Woodhill Farm co-owner/manager Allan Cahill points out:

"There's a fine balance between what works for cows, and what works for the people taking care of the cows," he explains. "The fact is, the cows like the sand we put in the regular stalls the best. But it's expensive, it's labor-intensive, and it goes out with the manure, which complicates manure storage and spreading. It's also coarse, so it wears out your equipment."

So dairy cows like to sit in sand like they're in Jamaica. Who knew? But it's a pain in the wallet for their keepers.

"This is where the waterbeds come in," Cahill continues. "They're expensive to purchase and install, but once they're in place they are really easy to take care of. We just put some sawdust on them for traction, and they clean up comparatively easily."

As you can see, the waterbeds work on many fronts. The cows like them, they're low-maintenance, and they can be washed quickly, which is a boon to bio-sanitation and therefore cow health. What's wild is that the waterbeds really just look like concrete covered with sawdust until a cow steps on one, and then it moves like a waterbed. Oh, and to keep the beds from freezing in winter, they're filled with windshield-washer fluid. Through technology we have economic efficiency, cow comfort, and ultimately more milk and other good things. Connecticut dairy farmers rock, man.

They may look like regular cows, but these swingin' sisters are totally into waterbeds.

Here's an old Connecticut custom we think should be revived: bundling. When a young man and a young woman were trying to make a decision whether to marry, the idea of sexual compatibility was not overlooked. Oh, no. The two were allowed—under fairly strict supervision—to spend the evening together. In bed. Fully clothed. Often with a long board between them. Many times they were wrapped tightly in separate blankets (hence, "bundling"). Of course the overseers—usually one or both sets of the young folks' parents—had to sleep eventually. And boards can be removed, as can tightly wrapped blankets—and clothing. Oh, those nutsy, kookie Puritans!

The Serious Business of Puppetry

Mansfield

All right, class. Now lift the right arm! No, the right! The right! Don't you know anything?

The folks at the University of Connecticut's puppetry program and the Ballard Institute & Museum of Puppetry take their puppets very seriously. Besides stunning men and women's basketball teams, the school offers the only puppet arts training program in the country where students can earn an FBA, MA, or MFA.

It's not kid's play, either. Alumni have worked on Broadway (*The Lion King*), in Hollywood (you name it), and throughout the world.

The puppet program, part of the drama department, was started in 1968 by Professor Frank Ballard, who'd joined the faculty a few years earlier. It has expanded now to include classrooms, theaters, and a puppet lab where, twenty-four hours a day, students can build the perfect beast. They are encouraged to do that, in fact, and if you walk through the lab or anywhere near it you might hear the kind of frustrated cries any creator is subject to: "Damn these hands!" "My eyes won't work!" "I can't get her to stand straight!" Puppetry students are encouraged to mount at least one production in their UConn career; puppet classes are open to any UConn student.

The Ballard Institute & Museum of Puppetry is in Willimantic Cottage on Route 44 at the UConn Depot Campus—what was once the Mansfield Training School. Call (860) 486–4605.

Most of Ballard's puppets aren't nearly so static.

A True Cinematic Survivor

Mansfield

It's a curious thing when an icon of past popular culture stays around when many considered it to be obsolete. A perfect example is the drive-in movie. There are abandoned examples of these outdoor theaters all over this country. What's really weird is when you find one that is not only surviving but growing, expanding, and thriving.

The Mansfield Drive-In on Route 32 in Mansfield (860–423–4441, www.mansfielddrivein.com) was originally built in 1954 during what, we think it's safe to say, was the drive-in boom. In 1962 the outdoor theater changed hands and soldiered on weak knees until 1974, when Michael Jungden came in to manage the place. In 1991 he was able to make a down payment on the theater and take over the ownership.

All during this period, when the fortunes of most other drive-ins were fading away, Jungden kept the place going by making steady improvements and using the facility for flea markets during the off-season. He loves the place and intimately knows every aspect of its construction and operation.

"When I took over in 1974, the place was in pretty bad condition," he explains. "The previous owners pretty much went bankrupt, and things were in bad repair. I worked on it little by little, and the place started doing a little bit better year after year."

In 1985 Jungden put up two additional screens on the property, which made the Mansfield a three-screen drive-in. Three years ago he bought land adjacent to the theater and now has built facilities for an indoor flea market to keep things going no matter what the weather.

But he attributes the theater's success largely to his long, hard struggle to get first-run movies for his customers. "It took twenty-five years to get things to the point where the film companies will give us what we want when we want it," he says. "And now that there are so many great family films coming out, it's really been great for us."

What's this? A drive-in movie theater that's not abandoned and overgrown with weeds? There are a lot of kids that have never seen such a thing before.

A Ledger Becomes Linguini
Pomfret

New England, like so much of this country, is populated by folks who tend to find their own solutions to the problems that float across their transom. Sometimes they pass these solutions on to others, often making a successful business out of what was an answer to a personal need.

Walter Scott Jessurun was such a man. Well over a hundred years ago, he started a publishing concern in New York City that was based on a simple, elegant ledger he originally designed for himself, called "Beat Yesterday." This accounting journal was a super-simple way of comparing current sales with previous business, and he decided to sell his ledgers to other businesses—with tremendous results. Over the years his invention has been used by everybody from mom-and-pop stores to McDonald's and Wal-Mart.

A century later, it's clear that Brian, Barry, and Eileen Jessurun are definitely cut from the same cloth as the ancestor who passed down a successful family business. (The ledger itself lives on and is now also available in software form.) And like Walter Scott Jessurun, Brian, Barry, and Eileen found themselves faced with a problem and decided to create a solution themselves. In this case they wanted an affordable, high-quality cafe in the wilds of Pomfret so that they wouldn't have to drive miles to some enormous, crowded metropolis (like, oh, Putnam) for a decent meal. So they built the Vanilla Bean (860–928–1562, www.thevanillabeancafe.com). They had never attempted anything like this, so the project was doomed to fail, right?

No way, José. Like "Beat Yesterday," the place caught on and is now a wonderfully successful cafe with live music and a loyal following that includes everybody from local arts groups to motorcycle clubs. There's great food, a great atmosphere, and nice folks. Bottom line? Never doubt the creative abilities of a Jessurun.

Where The Wolves No Longer Roam

Pomfret Center

Some of Connecticut's most interesting history is hearsay—interesting tales that may or may not be true. And so we offer the following, with no claim as to the veracity of the tale:

In the winter of 1742–43, a wolf plagued the farm people around Pomfret. The animal, which had been able to escape capture despite once being caught in a trap, was said to have killed 70 sheep in one night. (See what we mean about hearsay?) The townspeople organized to catch the wolf—said to be a female—and traced her back to a den not far from the farmhouse of Israel Putnam, a local man who would serve with distinction later as a soldier and general in the French and Indian War and the Revolutionary war.

Dogs sent in to flush out the wolf returned badly hurt and refused to go back in, so against the advice of his neighbors and his servant (who refused to go in himself), Putnam tied a rope around his leg and crawled in. It took him three tries and one shot, but he was able to bring the wolf out, dead.

The townspeople were so happy (and so starved for entertainment) that they hung the animal's body from a spike at a local tavern and celebrated. And Old Wolf Putnam, who is credited with saying "Don't fire until you see the whites of their eyes" in the Battle of Bunker Hill, had earned his lifelong nickname.

The wolf den is in Mashamoquet Brook State Park, off Route 44 in Pomfret.

Connecticut hero Nathan Hale was captured by the British because, for all his enthusiasm, he wasn't a great spy. To aid the American cause, Hale, a Coventry native, posed as a school teacher in 1776—his job before the war—to get information from the British. He was captured and hanged without a trial, but not before he could say, "I only regret that I have but one life to lose for my country." He was twenty-one and a graduate of Yale University.

The Elusive Mrs. Bridges
South Woodstock

It was a long time ago—more than 200 years, in fact—when certain uppity colonists decided to thumb their noses at the British by hitting them where it hurts, right in the tea. They tossed the leaves that make the lovely beverage into the ocean, and ever since (with the exception of the Beatles and the Stones) this country has tried to distance itself culturally from Mother England.

But if you wander into the shop at 292 Route 169 in South Woodstock, you may just hear and see things that show you how much times have changed. Individuals with British accents are often heard mixing freely with Yanks; even more shocking, you will see them drinking (gasp!) tea. Not just any tea, either, but proper British tea with proper condiments and pastries.

Started by British-born Veronica Harris and Diana Jackson in 1992, Mrs. Bridges Pantry (888–591–5253, www.mrsbridgespantry.com) is a place where you can leave America and hang out in England for a while.

What started as a few shelves in an antiques store is now a store with nooks and crannies stocked with everything from British canned goods and candies to fine china, knickknacks and (of course) teas. Tables hide in a tiny tearoom where visitors enjoy fresh pastries and beverages, and one section is devoted entirely to the knitting trade.

The whole experience is wonderfully U.K., and this shop sells all the fittings you need to Britify your own pantry. A word of caution, though: Spend too much time here and you might find yourself riding your motor scooter home on the wrong side of the road. As for Mrs. Bridges herself, well, you can meet her as long as either Veronica or Diana is working the till.

"We took the name Mrs. Bridges from the PBS series *Upstairs Downstairs*," explains Veronica. "She was the cook in this great series. We both answer to the name Mrs. Bridges now, and we've had a few people come into the shop believing us to be a long-distant relative!"

Nothing like a spot of tea and scones.

The nutmeg seed—the part the Colonists craved—is encased in an apricot-sized fruit. It's a flavoring, it's an emetic, it's a hallucinogen. Malcolm X wrote in prison that one hit of nutmeg stirred into cold water had the "kick of three or four reefers." However, he also allowed that the high wasn't all that great. Nevertheless, nutmeg was the first global commodity. It seemed everyone wanted a hit. In fact, the nutmeg was so in demand that dishonest peddlers would substitute grated wood chips to unsuspecting Colonists, so maybe that sobriquet "Nutmeg State" isn't all that complimentary.

The Horse That Won the West

Storrs

In 1789 a Vermont schoolteacher named Justin Morgan was stuck with a small horse (about 14 hands) that no one wanted. The colt had come to him as partial payment of a debt. From its inauspicious beginnings as halfhearted payment, the colt, known as Figure, managed to earn the admiration of Randolph Center and beyond.

Figure pulled logs draft horses couldn't move. He gave a fancy ride to President James Monroe. He outraced race horses. He became so popular that surrounding farmers wanted him bred to their mares, and his offspring were as beautiful and no-nonsense as their sire. Eventually Figure became known as Justin Morgan, after his owner. Justin Morgan, the horse, died at age thirty-two in 1821, but by then his legacy had spread.

During the gold rush people rode Morgans out west. During the Civil War the U.S. government bred Morgan horses for the U.S. Cavalry. The lone survivor of the Battle of Little Big Horn was a Morgan named Comanche.

After World War II, however, the government decided to get into more dependable business than horses and gave their remaining Morgans to five universities, including the University of Connecticut. The modern-day offspring of Justin Morgan live at the stables along Horsebarn Hill, just off Route 195, which cuts through the Storrs campus.

Going for the Doggie Gold

Storrs

Ah, the unrivaled fanfare of the Olympics! The pomp! The circumstance! The great mutual respect among competitors as they strive to best one another on the field of play! Best of all, the cheers from the crowd when the bad guy is wrestled to the ground like an evil chew toy by a furious, attack-trained German Shepherd!

Sound familiar? No? Oh, you must be thinking about that other Olympics.

That's a great event, too, but in Connecticut the Olympics doesn't solely refer to competition among human beings. For ten years now, the Canine (or K–9, actually) Olympics have been hosted by the University of Connecticut Police Department. This police dog field competition is open to all full-time Connecticut law enforcement and correctional K–9 dogs—and, of course, their handlers (www.police.uconn.edu/k92.html).

It's quite a spectacle. The audience (which is usually around 2,500 persons) gets to watch the dogs compete at a variety of events, including an obstacle course, a building search, shooting exercises, and even a wild Criminal Apprehension Drill where the dog charges about 50 yards across a field to attack a gun-wielding "assailant" (who, thankfully, wears a padded suit). It's all in good fun, but it also demonstrates how well the cops and canines work as a team.

The Olympics are held every August, and souvenir and beverage sales benefit local charities. Best of all, this is one Olympics you can actually go to without flying halfway around the world.

Lost in the Dark
Thompson

As you may have noticed, we're really into mazes. We've experienced some pretty cool ones in the state already, and up in Thompson they have not only a truly singular maze, it's actually a member of a franchise of mazes that is spreading through America's cornfields. They're popping up all over, much like selectively hungry locusts eating their way through the kernels to create their own special brand of crop circle.

Located on the spacious Fort Hill Farm on Quaddick Road (860–923–3439, www.cornmaze.com), this northeast member of the Maize Quest network offers some weird and wonderful variations on your basic cornfield maze, including a theme for the field itself. In 2005–06, the theme was called Quest for Freedom, with the maze featuring clues and discoveries to educate visitors on American heritage while helping them navigate their way home. An aerial view of the maze revealed a bald eagle shape in the cornrows, so when it comes to having an all-pervasive theme these folks don't fool around.

But by far our favorite feature of this maze is that you can navigate it at night if you wish, provided you bring your own flashlight on selected nights. This makes the experience all the more surreal, and proves those who will challenge the maze only during daylight hours are wimps who can't truly achieve the level of Maze Master.

It should be noted that Fort Hill Farms has many other attractions just in case the corn maze is not your kettle of vegetables. These include some excellent gardens (called the Quintessentials) that include a Lavender Labyrinth with over 300 of the fragrant plants in a sunken garden. There's something here for just about everybody who likes growing things, for as we mentioned before, this is a very spacious spread.

The Fort Hill Maize Quest is a seasonal affair, typically running from mid-August to the end of October.

If you like a puzzle you can walk around in, have we got a cornfield for you!

Killingworth's Albert Buell was an engraver, silversmith, and inventor. He engraved the wall map that became the first one produced in the United States after the Treaty of Paris in 1783.

Would You Like Some Books with That?
Union

Not only do they encourage reading at the table at Traveler Book Restaurant in Union, they give you a free book—and sometimes more than one—with your meal to urge you along.

The restaurant was started in 1970 by Marty Doyle, an avid reader who one day brought a few books to the restaurant to give to a handful of valued customers.

Like any good idea, things got out of hand. Before long, Doyle was handing out a book with every meal. In 1993 Doyle sold the restaurant to first-time restaurateurs Art and Karen Murdock, a husband-and-wife team who knew not to tamper with success. Doyle didn't go far. He moved into the restaurant's basement to run—you guessed it—a bookstore of his own, but the Murdocks are still doling out books with cheeseburgers and turkey sandwiches. They find their wares at overstocked stores, library book sales, estate sales—and sometimes they even get donations from customers.

On a recent snowy afternoon, a young woman walked past a table of considerably older patrons, clutching four thick books under one arm. "Reading all those?" one of the older diners asked. "You bet!" the young woman replied.

For their book-a-meal policy, Traveler has garnered the attention of the literary world. Hanging on the walls are letters from writers such as William Styron and Dr. Seuss, who approved of the restaurant's marriage of commerce, food, and literature. Customers are free to pick their own volumes.

It should be said, as well, that the food's pretty good. The restaurant specialty is turkey. One year, Art Murdock says, they sold thirteen tons of the stuff. The restaurant is closed twice a year—Christmas and Turkey Day. Otherwise they're open 7:00 A.M. to 8:00 P.M. every day. The Traveler Book Restaurant is at 1257 Buckley Highway (exit 74 off I–84, for you highway types).

Take a gander at Traveler's basement bookstore.

The Night the Frogs Really Croaked
Willimantic

A local legend around Willimantic has it that residents, already jumpy about living out in the wilderness, were called out of their homes late one night in the very dry 1750s by the most horrible sound.

Some, more curious about the noise than modest about their covering, came out fairly scantily dressed—naked, even. But it was only the next morning that they discovered the source of the sound: hundreds of bullfrogs, dead from the drought. Of course word got around, and Willimantic became the butt of the joke.

Here a frog, there a frog.... In Willimantic, frogs rule.

So what did the citizens of Willimantic do to fight back? Embrace the frog, that's what. They put the frog in their town emblem; they placed it on the rings of their graduating seniors, and in 1999 they affixed four 11-foot, 2,000-pound bronze frogs atop spools of thread—the latter to represent the city's manufacturing history—across a whimsical $13.4 million bridge that moves traffic across the Willimantic River. You can't look at this bridge without smiling.

The frogs, designed by Ivoryton, Connecticut, pop artist Leo Jensen, were cast by Jozef Witkowski in his Bridgeport foundry. The concrete spools on which the frogs sit were made by the Coreslab Structures (CONN) Inc.

But Are Their Cords Long Enough?
Willimantic

Every year, while bombs burst in midair, the denizens of Willimantic form for their annual Boombox Parade. It's a combination birthday-party-Mardi Gras-anything-goes display of civic pride—and a perfect opportunity to abandon one's self-respect. It is one of the more popular parades in the state, with the help of local radio station WILI–AM (1400 on your radio dial) playing its daylong lineup of patriotic songs.

The parade began in 1986. Without a high school marching band, organizers decided to do the next best thing—bring portable radios and tune them to WILI. Over the years the parade has attracted an eclectic crowd—from people dressed as frogs to honor the town emblem to people dressed as giant carrots to puppeteers to you name it. Look for them marching down Main Street every July 4.

The Little Pink House of Mr. Fourth of July
Woodstock

During his life, Henry Chandler Bowen held fancy Independence Day parties for the likes of Oliver Wendell Holmes, Harriet Beecher Stowe, and Ulysses S. Grant, who must have hated his stay, because temperance-minded Bowen did not serve liquor.

Did President Ulysses S. Grant like the teetotaling Roseland Cottage? We suspect not.

Instead he served—to match the rather shocking hue of his house—pink lemonade.

Bowen, a silk merchant, was born in Woodstock but made his fortunes in Brooklyn, New York. He returned home to build his shocking-pink Gothic Revival cottage in 1846. With its green shutters to represent leaves, the place looked like a large wooden rose—or a fancy bit of pastry. No matter. Bowen was happy with the pink. It was a different time, you could say. A rich Victorian man could paint his house pink, and few would make mention of it—at least, not to the rich Victorian man's face.

The residents of the small farming community hardly knew what to make of it, or the ornate parterre—a garden planted in a pattern—he laid out in 1850. (That garden was restored in 1978.) Still, for twenty-four years, from 1870 to 1894, he was the town's (nonalcoholic) party animal on the country's birthday. Bowen also published a newspaper that pushed his Republican, abolitionist, temperance beliefs.

Roseland Cottage is at 556 Route 169 in Woodstock, and is open seasonally. For more information, call (860) 928–4074.

SOUTHWEST

Watertown

Southington

Minortown

Waterbury

New
Milford

Woodbury

Cheshire

Danbury

Newtown

Bethel

Redding

Shelton

Derby

New Haven

Orange

NEW YORK

Ridgefield

Stratford

Thimble
Islands

Bridgeport

Norwalk

Stamford

Long Island Sound

NEW YORK

0   10 Miles

0   10 KM

SOUTHWEST

Drive-in Time Machine
Bethel

Nostalgia is making a big comeback, and all you have to do to partici-
pate in the renewal of classic designs is buy a new car. The new Ford
Thunderbird, Chrysler PT Cruiser, and Volkswagen Beetle all hearken
back to a simpler, more stylish time (like the
1950s). The question is, as a person
concerned with maintaining
stylistic continuity, where
are you going to take
your new retro car
that is equally
nostalgic?

Please don't eat and drive.

The Sycamore Drive-In Restaurant, even beyond the neo-retro cars that often hang out in the parking lot, is a veritable time machine, with chrome bar stools and carhops. This is quite probably the oldest drive-in restaurant in America, and to walk through its doors (or order from your car) is to step back to an era when cell phones were found only on Dick Tracy's wrist.

"My family's only been running the restaurant for four years," explains owner Patrick Austin, "but the Sycamore has been in continuous operation since 1948. The recipes were handed down as the business was sold from family to family. This includes our root beer, which is a secret recipe, to the steak burgers, where we cut and grind our own fresh beef every day. This is not done much anymore these days, but the tradition here has continued since 1948."

From the decor to the cuisine, and even (amazingly enough) to the prices, this joint is a solid gold blast from the past. Located at 282 Greenwood Avenue (203–748–2716), this is a true drive-in where you can flick your headlights and one of the Sycamore's finest will come to your car and take your order. That goes for folks who drive twenty-first-century automobiles, too.

Ladies and Gentlemen, Suckers of All Ages
Bridgeport

You can find a lot to like about the Barnum Museum, but our favorite is the display that's a fake of a fake.

Former newspaperman P. T. Barnum quit journalism in 1834 and moved to New York City to become a famous carny, purveyor of hokum, master of nonsense. Perhaps even he didn't know how successful he'd be. He brought the world the FeeJee Mermaid—really, the carcasses of a fish and a monkey rather sloppily sewn together. What he told paying customers, however, was that the wizened, scary figure was an embalmed sea maiden bought near Calcutta by a Boston seaman. Even when people knew the thing was fake, they still came to his museum.

He also brought us the 161-year-old woman (give or take a hundred years), who claimed to have been the nursemaid for George Washington, whom she called "Georgy." Mostly, though, Barnum brought us the notion that if it isn't real, it can still be entertaining—maybe *especially* if it isn't real.

The museum was started with $100,000 seed money from the maestro himself in 1891. It was intended to be the Barnum Institute of Science and History, but it, like Barnum, got sidetracked. See the diminutive coach of little person and native son Gen. Tom Thumb and his wife, Lavinia Warren. Look, too, for the Brinley Circus, a scale model of a five-ring circus alive with swinging acrobats, performing horses, musicians, tents glittering with lamplight, sideshows, and a menagerie. The creator, Meriden's William Brinley, spent sixty years working on this model. Don't look for Jumbo, Barnum's famed "Largest Elephant on Earth." At the height of his career, that elephant was hit by a freight train. The remains went to Tufts University, where Jumbo was stuffed and displayed until 1975, when a fire destroyed the carcass. Now rumor has it that all that's left of Jumbo is stored in a peanut butter jar at the university's athletic department. And why not? It *is* Barnum, after all.

But mostly see the fake FeeJee Maiden. And this is what we like best about it: The modern-day FeeJee Maiden is a fake, too. The original probably burned with the museum in the 1860s. New York artist Stanton Kip Miller made the new fake one for an HBO special. But it looks real. At least, it looks as real as the original fake one did.

The Barnum Museum is at 820 Main Street. Call (203) 331–1104, or visit www.barnum-museum.org.

Paul Bunyan as Flagpole
Cheshire

He's the kind of figure that can give a man quite an inferiority complex. And while we do have our share of trees in Connecticut, it's not the kind of state you normally would associate with Paul Bunyan, the enormous lumberjack and beard-modeler.

But as you negotiate the wild woods of West Johnson Avenue in Cheshire, danged if you don't spot the giant Bunyan just after you cross Peck Avenue heading west. It's kind of startling, as you don't have a wandering 10-foot-tall Babe the Blue Ox to warm you up for Paul's arrival. What the heck is he doing here, in front of The House of Doors?

"Paul originally came from a tire store in Plainville," explains House of Doors owner Samuel Coury.

OPEN TO THE PUBLIC

HOUSE OF DOORS
LARGEST SELECTION OF DOORS IN THE U.S.A

You're going to tell Paul Bunyan he can't be a sign if he wants to be? I don't think so.

"The reason we have him now is that before we went in the door business we had a tree service. Paul Bunyan was sort of a symbol for guys that worked cutting down trees. As you might be able to figure out, he came to us in the late '70s, when some of the guys at the tire store needed some tree work done!"

Paul is, of course, one of a vast army of "muffler men" that are slowly but surely taking over the country. These guys were built mostly in the 1950s to hold giant mufflers outside normal-sized muffler shops—and terrorize people into fixing their exhaust systems. The House of Doors Bunyan is a bit unique, though, because he's actually a flagpole.

"There was a debate when we brought him here to Cheshire as to what exactly he was," says Coury. "There's a limit here as to how tall signs can be, but there's no limit to how tall a flagpole can be."

So you'll notice that Paul is always holding Old Glory as he gazes over his domain in Cheshire. I guess there's no muffling patriotism.

"Pop" Goes the Culture
Cheshire

Want your kids to grow up safe and strong? Buy them action figures by the dozens. OK, that's an oversimplification. But when Herb and Gloria Barker started allowing free tours through their Barker Character, Comic & Cartoon Museum, they hoped that children would see that there are other, saner ways to spend their time. Like collecting Psychedelic Pezes (there's a whole PEZ Room in the museum), or a vintage Yellow Kid gum dispensing machine. Or a California Raisin board game. (Bet you didn't know Elvis had one, too.)

You name it, the Barkers have collected it. Their museum is a veritable temple to pop culture—Kermit telephones, Superman telephones, one of the Seven Dwarfs telephones (Happy, maybe? Doc?). The museum has recently been expanded, but still has the feel of a very cool toybox. And when you're done looking at the not-for-sale stuff, the for-sale gallery is equally impressive. The art's not bad.

Admission is free. The Barker Character, Comic & Cartoon Museum of Memories is at 1188 Highland Avenue (Route 10). Call (203) 699–3822, or visit www.barkeranimation.com.

Sorry, no pictures inside, but there's loads of things to snap outside.

Mad as a . . .
Danbury

At its height in the 1880s, Danbury—also known as Hat City—was home to thirty or more hat-making factories. It was, suffice it to say, the hat-making capital of the world, and for a time one lit sign pronounced that "Danbury Crowns Them All."

The process of making a hat included something called "carroting"—or washing animal furs with an orange-colored solution that included mercury nitrate. Over time—at not much time at that—exposure to the compound attacks the nervous system, and leaves the afflicted person with symptoms similar to that of being drunk. For a while, such symptoms were called the "Danbury shakes." You don't hear that phrase much now, but "mad as a hatter" has stuck. (Lewis Carroll borrowed it for *Alice in Wonderland*.) After labor unions complained in the early 1900s, another process for preparing animal fur—which didn't use a mercury compound—was introduced. As a testament to hats' influence on the town economy, a derby hat adorns the town seal.

The mat hatters of old may be gone, but the mercury, say scientists, has sunk into the sediment. The Danbury Museum & Historical Society operates the John Dodd Hat Shop, built in the late 1700s. For more information, call 203–743–5200, or visit the Web site at www .danburyhistorical.org.

P. T. Barnum's Jail Cell

Danbury

First things first: It's not every day that you see a senior center with bars on the windows. Granted, it might not be a bad idea. The last thing we need is roving gangs of geriatric thugs tipping over mailboxes, drag-racing their walkers, and looting pharmacies.

But while the Danbury Senior Center at 80 Main Street (203–797–4686) does indeed have bars on the windows, it's not to protect the community. It's because the building is Danbury's Old Jailhouse, a facility that, it is said, once kept P. T. Barnum briefly incarcerated. In fact, Joel Benton's excellent book on Barnum has the circus giant stating that he was busted for libel and sentenced to sixty days in the Danbury Jail, where he lived quite comfortably and conducted business as usual. But some folks doubt Barnum's tale.

Did this senior center once house a dangerous criminal?

"I don't really think he was ever actually in jail here," opines the senior center's Mary Stalb. "I know there's a lot of nonsense about that but I don't believe he was ever really incarcerated here, even though the story has been going around for a long time."

Connecticut's Favorite Milk Run

Danbury

You're a lean, mean cruising machine—a biker of stature among your peers. When you and your crew get ready to go on a run on a sunny Sunday afternoon, where are you going to go?

Well, If you're like a lot of other New England bikers, you want to aim your headlight towards some smooth, curvy scenic roads that ultimately take you to a place where the refreshments are cold and the crowds are motorcycle types like yourself. No question about it: You need to ride to a dairy. A huge ice cream sundae, a cold shake, or some chocolate milk really hits the spot after a long, hard day of carving up the road with the thunder of your mighty steed.

Right?

In the case of Marcus Dairy Bar Restaurant at 5 Sugar Hollow Road in Danbury (203–748–9427), absolutely. What started as just a simple Sunday ride by a few guys from New Canaan has become the most popular weekend motorcycle hangout in New England. But how the heck did a simple cafe at a dairy that's been supplying Connecticut with milk for nearly a century grow into a two-wheeler Mecca?

"It actually started in the late '60s," explains Marcus Dairy's Sean Marcus. "Guys started riding here because the roads to the dairy were great, and the restaurant had big glass windows out front so that while they got a bite to eat, they could make sure nobody would mess with their bikes."

Now on Sunday (when the weather is decent) the dairy's parking lot is filled with motorcycles from all over New England. In the past the establishment would hold quarterly "Super Sundays" at which vendors, contests, and thousands of motorcyclists would cover the property. But parking (even for motorcycles) became such a problem that the events were discontinued. This shouldn't stop you and your riding buddies from stopping by, as the restaurant is still there with many of the original patrons still making the run.

The Hardware Store as Historical Treasure

Danbury

Ah, the neighborhood hardware store. It's not just a vanishing fixture of small town America, or just a place to find that elusive solid-copper toilet valve you've been searching for like it was some sort of plumbers' Ark of the Covenant. No, if you're lucky (or just live in Danbury) your hardware store is a registered National Historical Place.

Meeker's Hardware at 86 White Street (203–748–8017) is such a store; in fact, it's the only hardware store in the country that is certified as a historical treasure. This is largely because it has been in its present location since 1889, and the family (through five generations now) has been taking care of the feed, hardware, and tool needs of the working community for more than a hundred years.

The monument in the front of the store is a part of the building's heritage, for it used to be found on the fourth story facade of the building as it stood until 1896. A fire that year destroyed the top two stories, and the stone was buried in the rubble and wasn't discovered until an excavation of the basement in 1976. The original two stories remain to this day, and despite the aura of historical holiness Meeker's is still a down-home place where you can score that evasive nut or bolt.

"My husband's grandfather built this store in 1883," explains Lucille Meeker, "and it was feed and grain mostly. We still sell hay and bird-seed, but when the farms left we evolved almost completely into hard-ware. We still sell woodstoves, honey, whatever people need, like a general store. You can still buy nails and things by the pound here, too. You go into a modern hardware store and you have to buy them by the package."

From hay to history, Meeker's has what you need.

ART DECO TO GO

Between 1934 and 1940, the 37½-mile Merritt Parkway, named for Schuyler Merritt, a state congressman from Stamford, was built at a cost of $22.7 million. It was meant to ease congestion of the heavily traveled U.S. 1, also known as the Boston Post Road.

It did that—but it did more. It also showed travelers that a highway could be beautiful. In addition to what is known as a "ribbon park" that threads alongside the road, the highway was the product of landscapers, sculptors, and architects, among them George L. Dunkelberger, a Highway Department draftsman who designed the sixty-eight bridges that brought the highway national attention.

His Depression-era budget was small, so he used the very pliable concrete to his advantage. Some of the sixty-eight bridges have Gothic touches. There are wings on one in Stratford, relief sculptures of Native Americans in Norwalk. All carry at least a hint of the Art Deco design popular at the time.

But what is a pretty bridge if you're cruising by at 70 mph? The original speed limit was set at 45 mph—to allow travelers a chance to enjoy the ride and the view.

Strangers at the Station

Danbury

At first glance, the Danbury Railway Museum looks like an appealing little facility that chronicles the history of rail travel in this charming Connecticut city. That's exactly what it is, too.

But there's something a little weird about the place. In fact, you might get a creepy feeling that you've somehow seen it before. Lest you think this is a genuine case of déjà vu, you should know that your strange feeling of unspecified remembrance is cinematically derived (especially if you're a Hitchcock fan).

Today the historic Danbury Station at 120 White Street (203–778–8337, www.danbury.org/drm/museum.htm) may be the location of the Railway Museum, but fifty years ago it was a key location for one of Hitchcock's most memorable films, *Strangers on a Train*.

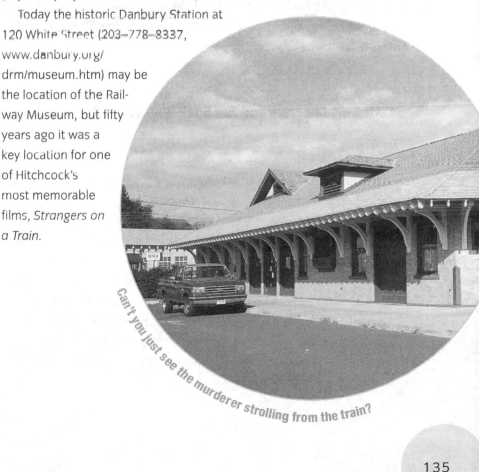

Can't you just see the murderer strolling from the train?

The year was 1950, and Hitchcock renamed the station Metcalf for the film, which starred Farley Granger and Robert Walker. The train station was critical to the story, as Granger and Walker meet on a train and this chance encounter results in murder with a very original version of blackmail thrown in. Toward the end of the movie, an important scene featuring Walker trying to fish Hitchcock's Maguffin (in this case a cigarette lighter) out of a storm drain was also shot right in front of the station. Hitchcock also carefully chose the garbage placed in the drain for the shot.

The museum has a display with some great production photos from the film in addition to some great exhibits of railroad memorabilia, including a huge selection of lanterns. A tour of some classic railroad cars is available as well.

Listen My Children, and You Shall Hear . . .
Danbury

. . . shockingly little about a young girl who rode three times farther than Paul Revere through treacherous terrain. And, unlike her more famous counterpart, she never got caught.

In 1777, Sybil Ludington, then sixteen, volunteered to ride 40 miles to alert colonists around her family's grist mill that the British were ransacking Danbury. Her father, Colonel Henry Ludington, of Branford, had settled into the Hudson Valley, in what is now just over the Connecticut line in New York's Putnam County. Someone had to alert the troops. Sybil volunteered, and spent the night riding through the rocky land in a rainstorm crying, "Muster at Ludington's!" The troops assembled, marched to Danbury, and helped drive back British forces in a retreat that was disastrous for the crown.

But have you heard of Sybil? No, probably not. A few children's books mention her, and a few die-hard historians make it a point to call attention to her name. Because there's no documentation of her ride, some historians are hesitant to believe the story. But, as one local resident said, someone had to alert the militia, and no one's been able to prove Sybil didn't do it.

In the 1960s, an artist made a life-sized statue of the girl. It sits in Carmel, New York, on Lake Gleneida. A smaller version, donated in 1971, sits in a plaza in front of the Danbury Library, at 170 Main Street. For more information call the library at (203) 797-4505.

Just try to catch me!

Corral Those Monarchs!
Derby

They're light, move quickly, and have a certain flighty quality about them. They also usually are associated with positive things in life, because they are perceived as basically harmless to humans and wonderfully beautiful to behold.

But that's just one side of the story, and some might say this is pure propaganda. People like me see them differently. These wild, erratic beasts need to be corralled lest they get all uppity and stampede our homes, park on our flowers, and demand strong drink. Like nectar.

Granted, the reasons you think you need a butterfly garden at your house may be different from mine. We say lure them to a controlled area so that you can keep an eye on the rambunctious insects. You, on the other hand, may want to have more of them around your dwelling because they are lovely creatures. Regardless of your motivation, the Kellogg Environmental Center in Derby (203–734–2513, www .dep.state.ct.us/educ/kellogg/kec.htm) has done something unique. In honor of the tragic passing of young Laura Cournoyer (one of the center's regular visitors), the center has created a superb butterfly garden at the facility that is designed to be easily duplicated at your own home. Arrayed in a small enclosure are butterfly bushes, hyssops, sages, purple coneflowers, blazing stars, lavenders, yarrows, and many others. The center has diagrams of the garden you can take home to use as a template for your own personal butterfly habitat.

And do these plants (when all deployed together) do the trick and lure the flighty ones? Absolutely. In fact, on a summer day at the center, there is veritable conflagration of winged insects that might be engaged in shenanigans if they didn't have such a great gathering place to hang out at. Think of erecting such a garden at your home as a public service.

SOUTHWEST

A Very Bizarre Structure

Minortown

They call him Cadillac Joe because he is usually seen driving a Cadillac. He shuns the spotlight and is known to reside in Bridgeport and commute to the strange structure on weekends—an ongoing project that he has worked on for years.

Most people call the structure the "Stone House" because it is built predominantly of stone. It is a weird, imposing edifice with intricately set chimneys in very ornate, artistic shapes. The variety of styles at play makes this home on Route 6 between Woodbury and Minortown a site you can't miss as you pass by. It looks to be part church, part ski lodge, and part Roman temple. But the details of the house and its history are a little bit of a mystery.

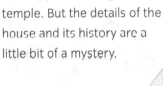

So what is it anyway?

The owner doesn't seem to crave publicity," says a Woodbury town official we'll keep anonymous. "He has been doing all the work himself, to my knowledge. A lot of the stonework is magnificent, too. The house itself is all steel-beam construction and there's a roaring stream out back, so there may originally have been a mill or factory at the site."

There is certainly a lot of industrial equipment there these days, such as a brace of bulldozers parked as though they are sleeping dinosaurs.

Flags by the Sea
New Haven

They were waving in the ever-present breeze that fills New Haven Harbor long before flags became omnipresent symbols of patriotism dangling from every other car antenna. The brightly colored banners that represent so many nations have become a fixture on New Haven's Long Wharf— and a great distraction for drivers rocketing down I–95.

He's called the Flagman, and he's been here just off the Long Wharf exit selling flags (and T-shirts, stickers, and other flag-related paraphernalia) since 1991. What is so unique about this particular vendor is not just his cool wares but the fact that he sells them in such a neat place, right on the water. It's a great choice, geographically speaking, because his goods are hard to miss from the highway and the breeze keeps them fluttering temptingly. The great diversity of designs is as varied as the cultures they represent.

Geography has been a big interest all my life," says the Flagman from the cozy comfort of his flag-filled van. "The business started basically with flags and a few other things of international and historic interest, with some military stuff."

It's an unusual specialty but an especially satisfying one because he's not just selling something cool to look at; a flag is an important part of a person's national identity. "We're really an international country, and we have a lot of people from other countries living here," he explains. "From time to time, everybody needs a slice of home, and I'm here to supply it."

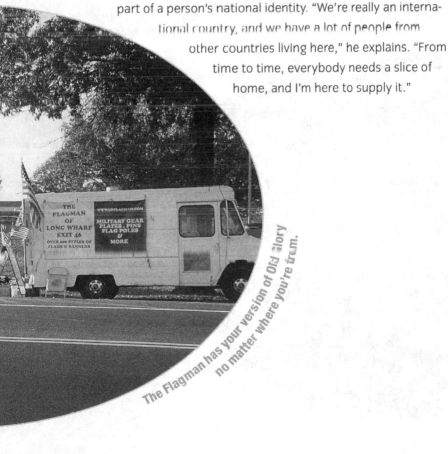

The Flagman has your version of Old Glory no matter where you're from.

WATCH YOUR LAWN FLAMINGO!

My friends, the purpose of this book is to enlighten and entertain, and to this endeavor we are truly dedicated. But at the same time, we feel compelled to remind you that we are also journalists and as such will warn you when we encounter dangerous curiosities of which you should be made aware.

Bottom line: Avoid the Southington/Meriden area at all costs. There, we've said it, and no doubt the publishers will be all over us on this one—not to mention a few Meriden Chamber of Commerce representatives. But we have seen evidence of great danger in these two communities, and we will not be silenced.

It all started with a visit to Hubbard Park, a really splendid pond/greenbelt combination in Meriden that has been offering residents respite from life's chaos since 1806. It was our intention to report on the really interesting Christmas decorations that adorn the park, because they really are quite striking and are even found in the pond (in the shape of geese) and in the trees (flying geese).

But then we saw the dinosaur tracks. Now, these dinosaur tracks are alleged to be very old, but to us there was something sinister about them. We are told that the species that likely made these impressions have been extinct for millions of years, even longer than the Rolling Stones have been making music. Yet, we felt uneasy. It didn't take long for us to understand these nervous misgivings. Some would say it had to do with the mysterious Black Dog of Meriden, which is said to curse those that see the animal in the area near Castle Craig. What nonsense! We think such legends are designed to distract people from the dinosaurs.

And there are dinosaurs in these parts, not just tracks. If you leave the park and access I–691 and then take exit 4, you will find, we believe, the creature that left the tracks in Hubbard Park. In a backyard easily seen from the Meriden-Waterbury turnpike you will in fact see . . . a dinosaur. Did this creature, now seemingly inert and composed of man-made materials, once stalk the park and no doubt threaten all the gnomes, lawn jockeys, and plastic flamingos in the region? We leave it for you to find the answers.

America's First Pizza Pie (Probably)
New Haven

All right, at least a handful of restaurants try to lay claim to the title, but we are officially giving it to Frank Pepe's Pizzeria of New Haven, home of the first pizza, ever.

Sure, everyone has his or her favorite, but at Pepe's they've been making pizza for seventy-six years, and they've been making it right. (The shop has a picture of former President Bill Clinton savoring a slice.)

No, we're not restaurant reviewers, but we know a good pie when we see and eat it. Try the white clam. No, wait. Try the sausage and pepper. No. No. Wait. Try the pepperoni. Or take a bunch of friends, and try them all.

Pepe's is at 157 Wooster Street. Call (203) 865–5762.

Treesus of Nazareth
New Haven

It's a cool little park that is very New England in character. This means it's small, has lots of different species of trees residing within, and is spiritually charged to the point where a religious shrine has literally grown out of the bark of a longtime resident that just happens to be a sycamore.

In this wonderful greenbelt at the corner of Chapel Street and Wooster Place near New Haven's Little Italy, devout souls started seeing the visage of Jesus Christ in the weathered bark of a special tree, said to be especially visible at night thanks to an electric light that enhances the visual spectacle. You're supposed to be able to see it in the late afternoon light as well, but the question was, which tree?

We asked one jogging coed who responded with "I have no idea." We were about to query an elderly couple, but the male member of the pair (who bore more than a passing resemblance to Alfred Hitchcock) glared at us in such a way that we thought conversing was not recommended.

Then it hit us: In order to have the spiritual experience, one needs to examine every tree in the park and let the inspirational chips fall where they may. This activity is highly recommended. In the broad assortment of woodsy textures I saw faces ranging from comedian George Carlin to actress Helen Hayes, but the Savior was more elusive.

Regardless, searching for Him is a great way to enjoy this lovely setting.

The trees have eyes . . . or maybe not.

Dem Bones, Dem Bones

New Haven

Beneath the busy New Haven green lie the bones of long-dead residents of New Haven, unmarked, and—generally—unremarked upon.

The seventeen-acre green—which was purportedly designed by Puritans anxious for a meeting place large enough for all the saved upon the Second Coming—was the town's first burial ground. Unlike today's neat rows of graves, New Haven's departed were placed wherever there was room, and only the wealthier could afford a stone to mark their grave. Sometimes people were buried on top of each other. The cemetery began to fill quickly after the yellow fever epidemic of the mid–1790s, and a new cemetery—Grove Street Cemetery—was commissioned on what was then the edge of town.

The green, which may have held as many as 5,000 final resting places, was still used as a cemetery until 1812, when Center Church was built.

When the church was built, the green's gravestones were moved to the new cemetery on Grove Street. New Haven residents and Yale students stood shoulder-to-shoulder to pass the stones to the new site.

But the graves remain. And the green is still one of the busiest plots in the state, as host to the annual International Festival of Arts and Ideas and concerts throughout the year.

Wait a second...who left the boots?

Anyway You Lick 'Em
New Haven

Among New Haven's many food-firsts (first hamburger, maybe the first pizza) is this dubious honor: first lollipop.

Roughly around 1882, George C. Smith of the now-defunct Bradley Smith Company came up with the idea of putting a hard, sourball-type confection on the end of a paper stick for consumption. Wherever he got the idea, a German employee of Mr. Smith's figured out a machine that would make the candies—called "Lollipops" after a popular race horse of the day. The machine turned out forty lollipops a minute.

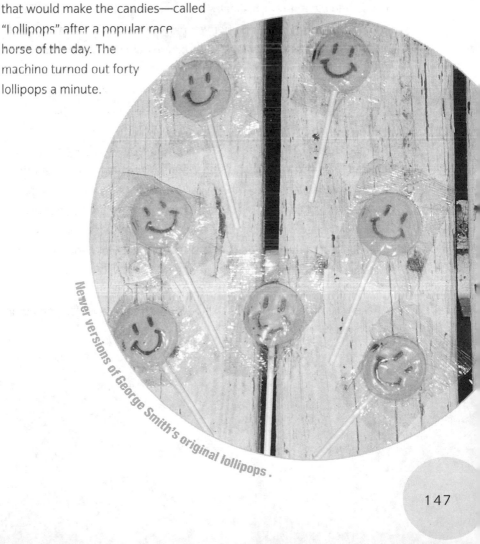

Newer versions of George Smith's original lollipops.

They Did It for Love

New Milford

Here's one story: Indian princess Lillinonah, daughter of Waramaug, grand sachem of the Pootatucks, found a handsome white boy—about her age—wandering lost in the woods. She took him back to her father, pleaded for his life, and eventually fell in love. By the first snow, she'd gained her father's consent to marry, but her intended requested that he be allowed to return briefly to his white family to tie up his affairs. He left, and did not return. Finally, Waramaug said that Lillinonah should marry a young Sagamore. On her wedding day, already bedecked in her finery, the princess pushed out in her canoe below the falls of the Housatonic River in the New Milford area and headed toward the rapids. Just as she was about to go over, her white lover appeared on the western precipice of the gorge and jumped 100 feet to his death to join her.

OR: In the late 1600s a respected sachem, Waramaukaeg, came to a minister's home in Woodbury to hear about Christianity. In the summer of 1687, the minister's seventeen-year-old niece came to visit. Waramaukaeg fell in love with her but could convince neither her nor her uncle that they should marry. One day the niece took a walk along the Housatonic, and the next day her bruised (but not violated) body was found beneath Bethel Rock. Nearby was the twisted body of Waramaukaeg.

Take your pick. Lover's Leap Bridge is south of New Milford on Pumpkin Hill Road.

SOUTHWEST

Bullet-Ridden Rooster
Newtown

Question: Why did the chicken cross the road?

Well, some believe it's to get to the other side, which denotes curiosity in some cultures. Others claim there was some distant feed involved, or perhaps a better life far, far away from the cruel fate that culminates in a bucket of Kentucky Fried Chicken.

Now that we've solved that question, another has surfaced: Why did the rooster climb to the top of the Newtown Meeting House? And where in the world did he get a Kevlar vest back in the 1780s?

The folklore that accompanies the rather handsome rooster weathervane is the stuff that legendary Revolutionary artifacts are made of. In a nutshell, so prominent and stately is the mighty rooster that back in the time of the American Revolution, a covey of inebriated French soldiers tried valiantly to dislodge the metallic cock from his perch with musket fire. It's a great story; however, historian Daniel Cruson thinks the shooters might have been Newtown residents, and so does the Meeting House's Sherry Paisley:

"I think the locals got into some White Lightning on a Saturday night and did the shooting," she says. "It was just sitting there, 100 feet in the air and had to be terribly tempting."

Indeed. Even after all this target practice (and more than 200 years later) this durable weathervane is still atop the equally durable Newtown Meeting House (www.newtownmeetinghouse.com). In fact, it has become the town symbol.

How the Other Half Lived (and How We, Even If Sales of This Book Skyrocket, Still Won't)

Norwalk

Bill Gates has nothing on the Lockwood-Mathews Mansion Museum in Norwalk. This nineteenth-century mansion is four stories high and features a huge octagonal rotunda surrounded by fifty decorated rooms. Yes, fifty. Craftspeople from Europe were brought over to create fresco, marble, woodwork, and etched-glass works of art throughout the building. For its time, there was nothing to compare (and certainly in our neighborhoods, there still is nothing to compare).

It's worth a visit just to see the setting of the Stepford Men's Association, from both freaky *The Stepford Wives* movies.

The Lockwood-Mathews Mansion is on 295 West Avenue (I–95 North to exit 14. Follow the ramp to West Avenue [first light], turn left, and proceed to the first driveway on the right after the turnpike). Phone is (203) 838–9799.

Your typical Connecticut garden shack . . . just kidding, of course.

Ol' Stew Leonard Had a Cow

Norwalk

In eight and a half acres of grocery store complex, you're bound to see some things you might not expect. That goes double for the long and winding aisles of Stew Leonard's—like, say a life-sized chicken, or a talking cow (named Wow) or a guitar-playing horse who strums the theme to *Deliverance.* This is the flagship store of a chain of three, and since it opened in 1969, Stew Leonard's has become a mecca for consumers.

Where else can you find mechanical vegetables and celebrity shoppers like Barbara Bush, Dolly Parton, and Henry Kissinger? Ripley's Believe it or Not named it the world's largest dairy store. The *New York Times* calls it the Disneyland of Dairy Stores.

Shoppers maintain a strange, cultlike devotion to Stew's. A wall is devoted to photographs from around the world, with Stew shoppers holding Stew bags in places as diverse as the Eiffel Tower and the Taj Mahal. Now that's product placement.

Want to visit Stew Leonard's? Bring a map.

Stew Leonard's main store is in Norwalk on Route 1, roughly 0.5 mile east of CT 53. Call (203) 847–7213, or visit www.stewleonards.com.

Have a Pfefferminz!
Orange

Today's lesson, class, is in Austrian history. In 1927 in Austria, an accomplished candyman named Edward Haas III marketed a tiny, compressed peppermint candy—a Pfefferminz. It was meant to be a mint for adult smokers, but when Haas brought the company to New York in 1952, he researched children's growing attachment to the tiny candy. Soon after, the company began to sell dispensers from which candy-eaters could gobble them—in an eerie manner, if you think about it. The dispenser head tilts back and out pops a candy.

But there's no accounting for taste (the Pfefferminz were not, after all, exactly Godiva chocolates), and PEZ dispensers are among the most popular of all collectibles. The candy company moved to Connecticut twenty years later, and now even the Orange-based company can't tell you how many dispensers they've, well, dispensed, but here's something you may not know: Dispensers sold before 1989 had no feet, so the dispensers could not stand upright on their own. Some of the rarer of these older models are the Baseball Glove, Batman with black hood and cape, and Captain America. (It's a PEZ rule that no living, real person can be made into a dispenser—a relief for those of us who wake up in the middle of the night fearing that very thing.)

Favorite characters have dispensed PEZ candies for decades.

Whatever the dispenser, the company says more than three billion of the candies—in orange, grape, lemon, and strawberry—are eaten annually in this country alone. Although the candies are made in Orange, the dispensers are made in Austria, Hungary, the Czech Republic, China, and Slovenia. Top sellers are Mickey Mouse (thought to be the first dispenser), Santa Claus, and, inexplicably, Dino of *Flintstones* fame.

Sadly, because PEZ is an FDA-regulated food plant, they don't give tours at Orange. Let your imagination wander instead, or visit www.pez.com.

On the Trail of a Literary Giant

Redding

As you may have noticed, Connecticut is very proud that Mark Twain (and Samuel Clemens, since they were one and the same) called the Nutmeg State home during different periods of his life. And although he is buried in Elmira, New York, he actually died here in Redding, at a home he called "Stormfield."

The name of the house comes from Twain's *Captain Stormfield's Visit to Heaven,* a small book he wrote around 1868 and the proceeds of which, it is said, helped pay for the land. Other accounts state that Twain originally planned to call the place something else, but decided to call it Stormfield after experiencing a particularly wild thunderstorm while visiting the property.

The structure itself was an Italian-style villa, and Twain didn't actually see the place until he moved in around 1908. He purchased the land and had the house constructed with the understanding that "I don't want to see it until the cat is purring on the hearth." His neighbors included Helen Keller.

Twain died at Stormfield in April 1910, and the villa burned to the ground in 1923. The town of Redding now owns the property around where Twain's villa was located (except for a private parcel around a privately owned home where the villa once stood), and visitors can stroll (or storm) around the Stormfield grounds on well-maintained hiking trails. This lovely outdoor recreation area may be the only one in the country named after a book that helped finance the land's original purchase.

To access the Stormfield trails, take Diamond Hill Road west off Route 53 in Redding. Take the second left (Fox Run Road), and follow it around and down the hill until you see the trailheads on your left.

The Bernese Mountain Dog Invasion
Ridgefield

They came in from the west, below our radar. Way below our radar, in fact. Sidewalk level, to be specific. They were well organized and orderly and brought entourages of human companions along with them. At first you think you're just seeing things, but then you realize there are far too many of these stately beasts marching along the sidewalks that line Main Street for this to be a mistake. Clearly, you've encountered some sort of Doggy Coup bent on taking over Ridgefield—or some sort of strange migration of big, beautiful canines from Berne, Switzerland.

Neither of these scenarios is accurate, for the Bernese Mountain Dog Invasion is simply an annual Ridgefield event that is done for the best of reasons: fun. We know this because we accosted a gentleman and his Bernese outside the Keeler Tavern, who told us, "Oh, there's nothing sinister going on and you're not seeing things. Every year we get together to walk with our Bernese Mountain dogs into Ridgefield, from a private home to the Bone Jour pet shop on Main Street" (203–438–1616).

Indeed, organizer Joy McMamigal says this is the seventh year the walk has taken place, and her family actually inherited the starting place for this walk when they purchased a house from the previous organizers:

"We just coincidentally happened to have a Bernese puppy when we bought the house from the folks that started this walk, and we agreed to continue the tradition," she explains. "This originally started with about ten or twenty Bernese Mountain dogs from the surrounding area, and now we're up to about one hundred fifty from all over. We even have one this year from Portland, Maine."

Cannon Balls at Happy Hour
Ridgefield

Picture this: You finally find that special watering hole you've been searching for all your life. The atmosphere is cozy, the bill of fare filling and affordable; best of all, the company is stimulating. Shoot, you've finally found people who share a lot of your views about politics, and you can discuss the issues of the day with a gaggle of sympathetic ears. Then what happens? The British attack and park a cannonball in the wall of your newfound home away from home. Typical.

This is sort of what happened at the Keeler Tavern back during the Battle of Ridgefield in 1777. In those days a place like the tavern was a very important gathering place in the community, as well as an important rest stop for travelers between New York and Boston. Times being the way they were, the British actually had the gall to make the Keeler a military target because of claims that the charming establishment was manufacturing musket balls. (Lest you think these were some type of Happy Hour cocktail snacks, we're talking about the round lead shot that was placed in rifles and fired at those nasty Redcoats.)

Long battle short: The Keeler Tavern survived the attack, and now, more than 200 years later, still wears a small cannonball lodged in a beam on the north side of the house as a badge of honor. A trip to 132 Main Street in Ridgefield can get you a tour of this historic saloon, complete with a docent in period garb and a peek at this rather unique Revolutionary decoration. Call (203) 438–5485 or visit www.keeler tavernmuseum.org for hours.

The Birth of Wiffle Ball
Shelton

At age twelve, Dave Mullany was a pretty good ballplayer, and that was saying something. Everyone in his neighborhood played ball, and games were fiercely played.

The problem, though, was there were rarely enough kids to make up two teams, and there weren't any full-sized baseball diamonds. As the kids got better, their hits went farther—into too many unsuspecting windows, if you were to ask the older neighbors with perhaps less of an appreciation for America's pastime.

To cut down on the broken windows, Mullany and friends improvised. They used a golf club and a plastic ball that wouldn't travel nearly the distance of a regulation baseball—or even a softball. They called a strikeout a "wiff," the approximate English equivalent of the noise a bat makes when it's swung, hard, without hitting a ball.

But that ball was wearing on Dave's young arm, so his father—also named Dave—perforated a plastic ball used in cosmetics packaging. After a lot of trial and error, father and son finally settled on a particular series of eight cuts in the ball, and Wiffle Ball was born. In 1953, the product hit the market. Today, all Wiffles are born in Shelton, along with Wiffle golf balls, Wiffle flying saucers, and Wiffle outerwear.

When Just Any Old Gift Won't Do

Stamford

If they don't have it at United House Wrecking, you need to ask yourself if you really want it. For example, where else can you get a winged horse sled, circa 1800s? Or a pair or marble *David* heads?

At United House, where there are five acres of antiques and junk, much of it salvaged from Gold Coast mansions. The place is particularly good for unusual furniture and garden statues, like the chicken sign that stands 2 feet deep, for only $135.

United House Wrecking is at 535 Hope Street. Call (203) 348–5371, or visit www.unitedhousewrecking.com.

Trash as Art

Stratford

It weighs a ton, looks like trash, and comes from your local landfill and dumpster. And it's not what you think.

The Children's Garbage Museum and Education Center is more than just a pile of trash. It's Trash-o-Saurus. It's the Connecticut Resources Recovery Authority's attempt to teach children the beauties of recycling, as well as reduce the amount of trash they produce. But the coolest part is what they do with the recycled trash. On tours, guides talk to schoolchildren about the amount of trash a person creates each day, say five pounds. For a class of thirty children, that's . . . wait, it's coming to us . . . 150 pounds of garbage a day.

And when the guides tell students that each person generates about a ton of trash a year, that really gets their attention. Especially when that ton is shaped into a Trash-o-Saurus. Created by Philadelphia artist Leo Sewell, Trash-o-Saurus is worth a drive from anywhere. Other exhibits along the tour, like the worm tunnel, where you can pretend to be a worm in a compost pile, were kid-tested before they were installed.

The museum is at 1410 Honeyspot Road Extension (off I–95, exit 30). Call (203) 381–9571.

If You Have to Ask How Much . . .

Thimble Islands

Of all the New England coastal states, Connecticut didn't get nearly as many islands as Maine, nor ones nearly as famous as Massachusetts.

But we do have our Thimbles, 365 of them just off the coast of Branford. All right, maybe not 365 except at the lowest of low tides, but that's the popular number bandied about by the boat tours that show visitors the islands. Once named the "Hundreds," the islands are thought to be named for the black raspberries—or thimble berries—that once grew there. English pirate Captain Kidd may have visited and hidden his ship in a natural harbor at High Island.

By the 1840s the islands were becoming a summer resort. By the turn of the twentieth century, the Thimbles had reached their golden age. Newspaper reporters prone to hyperbole dubbed the islands the "Newport of Connecticut." Boats from the Knickerbocker Yacht Club of New York made it a frequent stop, so did Yale's yacht club.

By the 1920s the islands had gone back to sleep. The Madison Avenue Presbyterian Church—which had given its facade for the construction of the *Hartford Times* building—still operated its summer camp there but closed it by 1928.

Today many of the thirty-odd islands that exist even at high tide don't have electricity. Some don't even have running water. About twenty-five are inhabited—from one-room cottages to a twenty-seven-room mansion. The largest is Horse Island, at seventeen acres, so named because a horse was once found there, supposedly a refugee from a passing ship.

Holy Land in Miniature
Waterbury

For nearly a half century, Holy Land U.S.A. has topped a bluff overlooking Waterbury as a miniature Jerusalem—about the right size for a population of Middle Eastern Barbie dolls. Along with a Hollywoodland-style sign comes a high-tech cross of steel that lights up at night—at one time in different colors, like purple for Lent and red for Christmas.

The park was the brainchild of attorney/evangelist and devout Catholic John Greco, who swore he was answering a call from God to rebuild Jerusalem in Connecticut. In the 1960s and 1970s, the ersatz holy city drew nearly 50,000 visitors a year. Today the parking lot gathers tumbleweeds, and the gates are chainlink and locked shut (although it's not very hard to walk around the gates for a closer look).

Since Greco died at age ninety one in 1986, the land has been held by the Religious Teachers Fillipini of Bristol. They've attempted to keep it up, but maintaining an entire holy city—even in miniature— is a tall order. Local Boy Scouts have contributed renovation of the sign for their Eagle Scout projects, but it's still pretty seedy. Few statues have retained their heads, and tiny replicas of buildings are missing or have been vandalized.

A pretty seedy-looking Holy Land U.S.A. sits behind a stone wall.

The park is closed, technically, and the nuns who control it discourage visitors. If you're interested, however, the defunct park is on Slocum Road. There's talk of rallying volunteers to fix it. We sure hope so.

It's No Waldorf, But . . .

Watertown

It's a curious day indeed when you realize that clothes do, in fact, make the man. We like to think we are defined by the content of our character and lofty things like that, but such is not always the case. If you're a wanderer with a penchant for moss in your interior decorating, folks may just define you by the clothes you wear. And if you happen to be a cave, you may find yourself named after the person in popular folklore that used you as a bachelor pad.

Leatherman's Cave is not exactly well marked, but we're pleased to report it's easy to get to. This beautiful little grotto is found just off Route 6 south of Thomaston. Head east on Park Road, and pull off to the left where you see

It may look a bit rustic, but to the Leatherman it was one of his more picturesque accommodations.

a trail leading off into the forest. When the trail forks, take the path on the right and in less than a quarter mile you'll spy Leatherman's Cave.

This pretty little shelter got its name from a famous wanderer who periodically called it home; a man who creaked when he walked because he was clad head to toe in leather. He roamed around New York state and Connecticut for many years, staying in caves and gaining legendary status until his death in the 1880s. Some say he was just a loner, others say he was running from a failed relationship that turned him into a hermit. Regardless, he had excellent taste in caves and has, judging by the abandoned sleeping bag we found near the cave's entrance, inspired a follower or two.

Gertrude's Most Singular Garden
Woodbury

In every field of endeavor, we've got to have our giants. Our wizards. The greatest of the greats. For example, those who appreciate architecture often worship at the altars of masters like Frank Lloyd Wright and I. M. Pei.

Given that architecture has its heroes, should it be any surprise that gardening has a superstar or two as well? Of course not. And Connecticut is one of the few places outside England where a garden exists that was designed by Gertrude Jekyll, a person most of the green thumb set feel was the greatest gardener ever to pull a weed.

Back in 1926 Gertrude was commissioned to design one of her gardens for the Glebe House in Woodbury (203–263–2855, www.the glebehouse.org). This house was (and is) a very special museum set up to preserve the dwelling originally built in the 1750s to house a clergyman, in this case John Rutgers Marshall. By the way, the name "Glebe" comes from the term used to describe the land given by the town to

Care to gad on the glebe? Here's the place to do it, mate.

their church leader. If one went "gadding on the glebe," it meant you were wandering around aimlessly on the farm of a clergyman.

Anyway, Miss Jekyll did provide a plan for a comparatively small garden, but her entire plan was not implemented. Why? Well, nobody seems to know for sure, but it was quite possibly economics that slowed the project, and then the plans may well have been misplaced. But in the '70s, the original plans were discovered and work began that continues to this day to ensure that Connecticut has its very own Gertrude Jekyll Garden. When we visited during the fall, though, the garden around the Glebe House seemed more Hyde than Jekyll, thanks to the invasion of autumn leaves. Take it from us: You'll be happier visiting during spring and summer.

Sculpture as Appetizer

Woodbury

It's amazing how something that's a little unusual can yank you right off the beaten track and into a dining establishment. For example, while minding our own business and sashaying (or motoring, as less artistic-minded types might say) down Main Street in Woodbury, we thought we saw something that was incredibly out of place. Where you would normally expect to see a garden-variety shopping center (with the usual shops and eateries), we spied a very futuristic version of Stonehenge that meant one of two things: Either there was a fresh round of UFO/Druid activity in this quaint town, or something *other* than UFO/Druid activity was going on in Woodbury for a change.

What was in fact going on was the worlds of art and fine dining crashing together on the lawn of the Good News Cafe. Renowned Chef Carole Peck has an art gallery in her restaurant to complement her award-winning menu of eclectic comestibles, and the art spills all the way outdoors. The lawn sculpture of George Nicke Hendricks has graced the cafe for a couple of years now, and the food (and art) within is as interesting and stimulating as the sculpture outside.

The Good News Cafe (203–266–4663, www.good news-cafe.com) is open every day but Tuesday.

Have you died and gone to Crystal Heaven?

SOUTH-CENTRAL

Wethersfield
Glastonbury
Rocky Hill

Kensington
Marlborough
Hebron

Cromwell
Salem

Middletown
Portland
East Hampton

Meriden
Middlefield

Moodus

Higganum
Haddam
East Haddam

Wallingford
Hadlyme

Deep River

Guilford
Madison
Clinton

0   10 Miles

0   10 KM

SOUTH-CENTRAL

The Red Bricks Are Coming!
Clinton

Proper building supplies can often be hard to find. Have you ever tried to build an igloo in Ecuador? It's practically impossible to locate all the snow bricks you need for a two-sled garage. Sometimes you have to improvise, and in so doing you might just create something out of something that's never been built out of that thing before.

Confused? This is understandable, but all will be made clear presently. The town of Clinton, especially the Historical Society, is very proud of the Captain Elisha White house and rightly so. It's a beautifully maintained structure that has a very unusual distinction. It is believed to be the oldest brick house in coastal New England. Built in 1750 by Captain Elisha White (no surprises there), the house was unique when first built because the red bricks used didn't exactly grow on trees in Clinton — or anyplace else in Connecticut, for that matter.

But being the crafty old seadog he was, Captain White is believed to have scored his bricks from a British ship, as it was common for vessels from the United Kingdom to use such heavy, stackable items as ballast. Some might have been leery of White's using these British transplants for building materials, as they could have been spies, but the captain soldiered on with confidence.

But imagine what a great emancipation it must have been for these Limey bricks! There you are, packed like sardines in the dank, smelly, rat-infested hold of a ship—thinking you will never again see the light of day and never again feel the crisp breeze blasting against your semi-porous exterior.

But now these bricks are not only free but are proud residents of a wonderful Connecticut community—and considered historically significant to boot. Not bad for a bunch of bricks.

So you think bricks don't get to see the world?

THE ANYTHING GOES CAR WASH

Anacleto "Nicky" Vento grew up in and graduated from a university in Rome, Italy. He taught school, immigrated to the United States, and opened up a garment company—and a couple of car washes. One, Classic Auto Wash, in Cromwell, remains today as a standard for getting the customer's attention. Located in this town just south of Hartford, Classic has a variety of figures and such guaranteed to make you pull over and think, "What is it about a large giraffe that makes me want to wash my car?"

No? How about a 20-foot-tall Santa, or a series of small lighthouses, or a collection of vintage gas pumps? Or a small but impressive collection of farm implements? Or a polar bear standing helpfully next to the car wash menu.

If it's roadside kitsch, Classic, at 23 Shunpike Road, (Route 3, near Routes 322 and 9) in Cromwell, has it. Visit them in cyberspace at www.classic autowashanddetailcenter.com.

What does Santa have to do with washing your car? Why, everything!

The Ivories of the Oak

Deep River

Just when you thought the remnants of the mighty Charter Oak (the tree that so cunningly protected the Connecticut Charter from British seizure in 1662) are exhausted, it turns out that there really was an amazing amount of wood on that sucker.

As you may have discovered elsewhere in this volume, the Charter Oak was felled by a storm in 1856. The story goes that the property owner commissioned John H. Most to build a piano for his daughters out of some of the wood from the famous tree, and in return Mr. Most could use the leftover wood as he pleased.

Mr. Most is believed to have built not one but three pianos out of the Charter Oak, cleverly spreading the tree's supply out by laminating parts of pianos with the Oak instead of building the entire instrument out of hardwood. One went to the three daughters, one went to the governor at the time, and one was ultimately retained by Most's family. A chair, chest, and all kinds of smaller items are claimed to have been made from the sacred lumber as well.

Please don't tickle the ivories.

Of these three pianos, we know of only one that is still intact and available for viewing by the public. Thanks to the Deep River Historical Society (860–526–1449), a genuine Charter Oak piano resides in the parlor of the historic Stone House on Main Street. But before you try to blast out "Maple Leaf Rag" on the instrument, be advised that it's way out of tune and should be left in peace.

"We have had it tuned in the past, but the tuners told us these square pianos don't hold their tune very well and it's best not to try," explains Curator Edith DeForest. "Tuning also puts too much stress on a fragile structure," adds the society's Jeff Hostetler.

You might not be able to play it, but you can certainly admire it; it is a very unusual piano made from Connecticut's most famous tree. The Stone House itself is also well worth your investigation.

Goodspeed's Folly
East Haddam

In the late 1870s, East Haddam had two ferry landings, one lower down the river than the other. As will happen anywhere, the ferry landing upstream was considered the upscale ferry landing, while the lower landing was for the common folk.

To bring more revenue to the area, shipowner William H. Goodspeed built a tall and gangly wooden structure at the lower landing on the site of his father's grocery store and named it after himself. Construction on the Goodspeed Opera House began in 1876: six stories and a hotel, the Gelston House, nearby. It was and remains the largest wooden structure along the 410 miles of the Connecticut River. If the snots wanted to land upstream at the Upper Landing, they'd have to arrange passage to the site of the arts factory with the most potential snottiness, the opera house. Goodspeed, faithful to his upbringing, included a country store within the building, where operagoers who took a notion could buy their notions, if you get the drift. It was also the post office, steamship arrival point, and office building. The theater opened in October 1877 and would eventually house not only productions and plays but also odd exhibits like the 65-foot, 75-ton embalmed whale Goodspeed brought in (at a cost of $5,000).

The building was high Victorian, and it looks something like a wedding cake sitting on the water. Some said it was overdone. In 1938 one reviewer called it "the most extravagant, the most impossible of all monstrosities disfiguring the river shores." But then, the theater had been empty since 1920, and it probably did look a little eerie. Eventually the state decided to tear it down to make room for a state garage, but historians and preservationists—including former Governor Abraham Ribicoff—helped save the building in 1963, and it's still the home of Broadway revivals, musicals, and other productions. It's come quite a way from being what a recent history of the place called "Goodspeed's Folly." There's been talk of building a new theater, but so far, the folly rules.

Come see for yourself. The still-active theater is on Route 82 on the east side of the Connecticut River. Call (860) 873–8668, or visit http://goodspeed.org for more information.

The folly still rules.

Just Keep Swingin'

East Haddam

Why, oh, why doesn't someone make a movie around East Haddam's swinging bridge? You won't find a neater one than this historic swing bridge. The steel structure, the longest such bridge in the country, spans the Connecticut River at one of East Haddam's prettiest points. The bridge, considered a marvel of its day, opened on Flag Day, 1913, and is still pretty splendid.

The middle portion of the bridge swings aside to allow boat traffic—mostly ocean barges and tall-masted sailing ships—to pass north and south. The bridge is extremely busy during the spring months, when sailors from north of the bridge are bringing their boats to Long Island Sound for the season, and in the fall, when they return home.

Each July, locals hold a Swing Bridge Celebration of the Arts. Come see the musicians, performers, artists, and craftspeople and, of course, the bridge itself in action.

East Haddam's pretty bridge just keeps on swingin'.

A Rose by Any Other Name
East Haddam, Haddam, et al.

Connecticut, the Land of Steady Habits, is known for all kinds of things, but we think it should be known in part for its loyalty to certain names—a loyalty that crosses boundaries and, at least in the south-central part of the state, makes maps wholly redundant. You have Haddam. You have East Haddam. You have Lyme. You have Old Lyme and East Lyme. In between, you have Hadlyme. Did anyone ever go out on a limb?

Not hardly. Early Yankees found a name and stuck with it. Haddam and East Haddam, which straddle the Connecticut River, were once the same colony. Haddam, the original name, may have come from Great Haddam in England. In 1754 the colony split (agreeably so, or so we're told). The folks in East Haddam liked the original name, so . . .

Freaky Demons
East Haddam

There's nothing like reports of man-tossing demons to draw a crowd, and Devil's Hopyard State Park has had more than its share of both. These East Haddam woods have loads of stories, starting back when the Mohegans and Pequots roamed here and ending with a more recent story—that of five guys who came to the park after it closed one night in 1999. At least two heard a whispered threat, "Leave now, or you'll join us forever," and then laughter. Another guy saw what he said was a beastlike demon sitting on a nearby fence. One guy claims he was thrown into a tree and that he later found four slash marks on his pants.

The region's Native Americans thought the area was the stomping grounds of a god, or Manitou. They repeated the story to the Puritans, who were not amused. The topography of the park is "typically New

England"—craggy granite rocks covered with moss and lichen, with the occasional babbling brook. English settlers thought the land wilder than average, the kind of land the devil would favor for a playground. Under Chapman Falls, where Eight Mile River drops 60 feet over granite rocks, are perfectly round holes created by rocks getting caught in eddies and being pounded for years by the rushing water. The natives were content to let those be a god's footprints. The Puritans turned them into holes punched by the devil's tail.

Reach your own conclusion—and find your own brand of fright—at the park 3 miles north of the intersection of Routes 82 and 156. Call (860) 873-8566 for more information.

The Slave Who Bought Himself

East Haddam

Like so many of his peers, Broteer, the son of a Guinea tribal king named Saungm Furro, was captured as a young boy by slave traders and brought to Rhode Island.

In 1750, at age twenty-one and having taken the name of Venture Smith, he was sold to a Stonington man, and then sold to another man who let him buy his freedom for just more than seventy-one pounds in 1765. An astute businessman, Smith eventually was able to buy the freedom of his wife and children, as well. Smith couldn't read or write, and he was often destitute, but over time he came to own a large farm, three houses, a vessel fleet, an orchard, and a fishing business. One son fought in the Continental Army.

Smith died in 1805 a highly respected man.

Every year in September, the month of his death, his descendants—many of whom still live in the state—meet at his East Haddam grave to commemorate his life.

We're on the Road to Nowhere

East Hampton

The much-famed Comstock covered bridge crosses the Salmon River, but it doesn't do anything but cross the river. This historic Howe-truss bridge is more of a scenic spot, left over from a busy spot. Built in 1873, the bridge was the only link between East Hampton and Colchester. Before the bridge, wagons (and pedestrians and horses, too) forded the river as best they could. That was no big deal in the dry summer months, but in the spring, when snow runoff swelled the brook, getting to the other side of the Salmon River proved to be some challenge.

Sure! You can cross the postcard-pretty Comstock Bridge, but why?

It was named after a former local postmaster, Franklin G. Comstock, and the bridge is in remarkably good condition. Town legend has it that during Prohibition, a truck loaded with illegal hooch once struck the side of the bridge (driver sampling the wares, perhaps?) and the expensive (and beloved) liquid began seeping into the stream. Fortunately, civic-minded residents rushed to the scene with buckets to rescue the stuff.

The bridge was closed to vehicles in 1932 and was left to rot when the state built Route 16 to take the place of the dirt road that snaked through the structure. A few years ago the Chatham Alliance of Resources, a group of several area civic and fraternal organizations, revamped the bridge and the surrounding area. Vandals occasionally mar the wooden structure, but it's still a beautiful place to come enjoy a picnic.

By the way, the fishing in the area isn't bad, either. Tastes run to trout, but the big catch around the covered bridge is, as you might expect, salmon.

"Star Dust"
East Hampton

At the turn of the twentieth century, the shoreline of East Hampton's Pocotopaug Lake was dotted with resorts, dance halls, and champagne breakfasts that attracted the movers and shakers and a few celebrities. At one point, a local newspaper breathlessly reported that Miss Frances Upson, leading lady in the Gershwin Broadway show *Girl Crazy*, was staying with her mother at the Clearwater Lodge. That's the show that gave us "I Got Rhythm," "Embraceable You," and "Fascinating Rhythm." Rumor has it that Hoagy Carmichael either wrote or was inspired to write "Star Dust" at an East Hampton hotel.

WITH A NAME LIKE THAT

About that name: East Hampton's Pocotopaug Lake was for years known as the safest lake around (never mind that in recent years the lake is better known for its fish kills). The name is Native American Wangunk for "divided Water." Legend has it that the Wangunks decided they had lost too many braves to the clear waters. A medicine man suggested they sacrifice the chief's daughter—named either Na-Moe-Nee or Cochica—to the waters. The story varies, but the young woman is supposed to have thrown herself off the lake's eastern bluffs and died, her death bringing calm waters. No drownings were recorded in the lake until a young man slipped through the ice in 1885.

Roadside Art, Part One
Glastonbury

Sometime in the spring of 1989, someone concerned that the state had destroyed wetlands to build a highway overpass stuck pink plastic flamingos into the drain pond at the overpass off Route 2 between exits 5D and 6. Pink flamingos may fly (so to speak) in other parts of the country, but they are emphatically not indigenous to the land of Ralph Lauren and weekend homes.

Nevertheless, someone claimed credit for the placement of the birds with an anonymous letter sent to Peter Pach, a columnist at the *Hartford Courant*. "We were poking fun at the ecological value of these highway synthetic wetlands and suggesting that this particular species of wildlife may be all that will thrive in the new habitat," the letter said. This particular species has more than thrived. The flock has, at different times, included as many as five flamingos—four pink, one a neon green. It has also been joined, at times, by a lobster trap, a plastic shark fin, and a white flamingo.

Technically, the people who place these oddities in the pond are trespassing, but no one has the heart to hassle whoever's doing it. In fact, a home video of someone wading into the water and placing a flamingo in the shallows was once delivered to the Glastonbury Chamber of Commerce. The picture was grainy, and no arrests were made.

The flamingos and their friends are usually gone by fall but reappear like the swallows at Capistrano come spring.

The Caffeine Aerodome
Guilford

True confession time: your authors have never been fond of airline seats. We have collectively damned the on-board furniture, and swear that various back ailments have come not from trying to lift things like woodstoves or printing presses, but instead from commuter flights that get stuck in endless holding patterns.

That's why we were shocked to discover that there is a venue at which airline seats somehow become comfortable. Not only that, they actually add to the ambience of what is already a pretty cool little coffee shop/eatery. Café Grounded at 20 Church Street in Guilford (203–453–6400) is ideally situated in half of a Quonset hut (the other half is appropriately appropriated by an art gallery).

Enter an era when air travel was not only cool, it was stylish.

There is a very chic airline art deco motif, so you get the sense you're on a Boeing Stratocruiser circa late '50s–early '60s. Upstairs you find the airline seats. A word to the wise: Seat 11B is ideal for that ideal "watching who comes up the stairs next" position that can make spotting Guilford's art elite a piece of cake. Or, it can make spotting Guilford's art elite a bite of a blueberry muffin, which we highly recommend. Specify toasted, with butter, and you will climb above the clouds of gloom and see the sun again. No, really.

Other excellent fare includes the coffee itself, which beats the battery acid found on most airlines like a rented mule. If breakfast is your bag, check out the four-egg B-52 omelet, which will let you go on for miles without refueling. There are some tempting crepes and other breakfast goodies as well, and an impressive lunch menu. Hey, those expecting airline food will be disappointed, and quite possibly well fed.

Some Things Age Rather Well
Guilford

Now here's something you don't see every day: a lovely, rustic, yet almost contemporary-looking house (and a study in stone masonry) that is more than 360 years old.

Holy cow! Makes you wonder what kind of shape the plumbing is in.

Well, since plumbing was something akin to science fiction back in 1639 when the Henry Whitfield House was constructed, you don't have to really concern yourself with it. But this attractive house on 248 Old Whitfield Street in Guilford (203–453–2457, www.chc.state.ct.us/whitfieldhouse.html) has the distinction of being the oldest house in Connecticut. So when your neighbor complains about his water heater problems and how his system was installed "in the Stone Age," be advised that he is exaggerating; his house is a mere pup compared with the Whitfield. In other words, he should stop complaining.

As for the old stone house itself, it's a perfect example of architecture that never goes out of style. When the house was built, the town of Guilford was just getting established and was inhabited mostly by Puritans who were fleeing religious persecution back in Mother England. Henry Whitfield was Guilford's first minister, and the house served for a while as a tiny house of worship as well as a defensive stronghold if needed (thanks to that sturdy stone construction).

As you can imagine, the house was home to many, many families after Whitfield left in 1650, until the state acquired the property back in 1900. Today tours are held for the public and the house is stocked with all kinds of interesting furniture and artifacts from Colonial times.

The Whitfield house is nearly 375 years old. Yikes!

Rocks in Concert

Haddam

At first we thought they were hitchhikers. Then we thought they were convicts, or possibly rogue members of a local rock band out cleaning a section of highway that they had "adopted," probably without state endorsement. As we looked closer, though, we were sure that these young people were clearly involved with some type of organized outing. These kids had notebooks and seemed to be paying particular attention to the surface of the numerous "cutouts" along the highway where construction crews blasted rock hills in half so that Route 9 could continue along in a relatively flat manner. As these youths with their stationery were clearly interested in the walls themselves, were they unusually well-equipped graffiti hooligans, scouting for a later roadside assault with their paint cans?

Even the rocks in Connecticut have a story to tell.

181

Thankfully, they were not. They were actually college students, who were examining the geological wonders that line each side of Route 9 (especially in the Haddam region). If you examine the cutouts along this road, you do indeed find some beautiful examples of sedimentary rock strata that are intriguing to behold, even if you care not a whit about geology.

Layers of schist and gneiss are clearly delineated and when mixed in with other rock strata, make the surrounding walls look like some bizarre layer cake as you motor along. This is especially striking considering that you don't see a lot of these displays in other parts of Connecticut. The only thing missing from this region is the geological structure known as an alluvial fan, as with all this schist everywhere we could see a very real case of the schist hitting the fan, scientifically speaking.

Murder in Motion

Haddam

There's nothing quite like an ocean cruise, unless it's a freshwater river cruise, where the waves tend to be much smaller. Also, when steaming down an inland stream (like the Connecticut River) you can enjoy a leisurely dinner secure in the knowledge that attacks by giant squids (which usually gobble down most of the abovedeck structures before sinking the vessel) are fairly rare. Ships hardly ever hit icebergs, and being plundered by Jamaican pirates is practically unheard of.

However, there is the distraction of . . . murder.

How inconvenient. It's a true hindrance to one's peaceful repast when the lights go out and somebody is done away with in the dining area, but there you go. Weird occurrences such as this are commonplace on Camelot Murder Mystery Cruises (800–522–7463, www.camelotcruises.com). In fact, you pay for the privilege of sleuthing while you violently gobble down an entree, like the ground-bound giant squid you are. As a diner/passenger, you are encouraged to interrogate witnesses, gather clues, abuse condiments, and find the killer as your dining companions are supplemented by either professional actors or hired assassins; we can't remember which.

A three-hour cruise will leave you satisfied calorically and entertained at the same time, in what has to be one of the more bizarre dining experiences you'll find anywhere.

My Dear Watson
Hadlyme

William Gillette was the son of a U.S. senator and was urged onto the stage by Hartford neighbor Samuel Clemens. He wrote plays and trod the boards, as it were, but Gillette was most famous for his portrayal of Sherlock Holmes, then a huge favorite of the playgoing public.

He worked in New York but returned to Connecticut every chance he got. In 1914 he began what would be a $1 million (no chump change then) five-year project of building a castle on the shores of the Connecticut. The building was, for its time, an exercise in modern conveniences and odd shortcuts that only a bachelor living alone could dream up. Chairs were mounted on runners so that diners could push back without scratching the floors. Doors were held shut—even closet doors—by elaborate locks, the workings of which were known only to Gillette. Fieldstones made towers and parapets that looked, from a distance, like melted wax. A small train ran guests throughout the wooded acres.

The place was, let's be honest here, rather ugly, but Gillette's company was so valued that he rarely had a weekend devoid of houseguests. Gillette died in 1937, childless and no less weird for his maturity. His will directed that Gillette Castle not fall into "possession of some blithering saphead who has no conception of where he is or with what surrounded." The train went to Lake Compounce, America's oldest continuously operating amusement park, in Connecticut. All that remains are a few bridges and trestles. The state bought the estate to use for a park in the mid-1940s. Although the castle is often closed for repairs (the place is not watertight, for one thing), visitors (some 300,000 a year) can still get close enough to wonder: Did the sapheads win out in the end?

The castle, on a 184-acre estate, is off Route 9 (heading north) at Route 148. Follow the signs, or call (860) 526–2336.

Roadside Art, Part Deux

Hebron

This is not the Mother Road, the Route 66 of jazz-song fame, but for a 38-mile-and-some-change route through Connecticut, Route 66 is pretty funky. Roadside art like Eagle Rock, halfway between Marlborough and Hebron, abounds.

Eagle Rock, a jutting rock painted to resemble an eagle's head, probably started out painted as a frog. In the 1970s the frog became a snake, but townsfolk seem to prefer feathers over slime.

Along Route 66 in Connecticut are countless examples of arts-in-the-woods. Eagle Rock has been most recently painted by the son of a former area probate judge.

Cultivating Sundials

Higganum

As you may have discovered through your careful, methodical perusal of this volume, New England in general and Connecticut in particular used to be very closely involved with measuring time. As the Clock and Watch Museum in Bristol shows us, Connecticut and Massachusetts used to be major clock/watch manufacturing centers, but that has all fallen by the wayside.

But never doubt the entrepreneurial spirit of this state. Hey, we may have lost the watchmaking industrial base, but some clever folks have actually figured out how to grow sundials. Or at least we *thought* they had, until we figured out that the sundials were actually inorganic in nature and served as decorative ornaments in some beautifully landscaped gardens. Oops!

Where some hedges look like sundials. And some sundials are sundials.

But our trip to the Sundial Gardens in Haddam (860–345–4290, www.sundialgardens.com) was not a wasted journey in the least. The gardens themselves do, in fact, feature some really beautiful sundials, but spend too much time trying to figure out what fertilizer they used to grow these ancient, solar-powered timepieces and before you know it, it will be dark. Then you would have missed strolling through some truly wonderful and ornate gardens, and that would be a shame.

The Sundial Gardens is a setting that since 1976 has featured formal gardens along with a tea and gift shop. These folks not only know their gardens, they really know their teas and regularly hold formal tastings. Located well off the beaten track in the Higganum section of Haddam, here's a place where you can enjoy an unusually good cup of tea in a garden where the only way of tracking the passage of time is the sun. Watches? Clocks? Who needs 'em, anyway?

The Hedgehog, Tootsie, and Old Big Jim
Kensington

You know, there are a lot of really great parks and hiking trails in Connecticut, and if you take advantage of them you will see a dizzying assortment of flora and fauna. These might include the American robin, our State Bird; the mountain laurel, our State Flower; or the sperm whale, our State Animal.

That last one is rare, especially on well-traveled trails, but you never know (if you can't find one in the bush, we can steer you toward a concrete version in West Hartford).

However, if you want to see something really unusual, exotic, or downright strange, only one park has something as common as a rabbit in the same room as some massive iguanas, a sleek chinchilla, and a hot, sexy young tortoise. The Park is Hungerford Park, and it's here where you'll find the "woodsy" division of the New Britain Youth Museum (860–827–9064, www.newbritainyouthmuseum.org).

This is a very special place, one where animals that might otherwise be done for get a new lease on life, thanks to the care and expertise of the staff. Many of the park's more exotic residents were pets that became unwanted when they became too large or people got tired of them. How anybody could grow weary of a pygmy hedgehog is a puzzle, for it's quite a lovely creature, but there you go. Other animals are injured and couldn't survive on their own, such as the park's red-tailed hawks and great horned owl, which have damaged wings.

There are also some particularly plucky farm animals that visitors are encouraged to meet and greet, and for kids living in an urban environment, a steer like Big Jim can be a great introduction to something larger and grander than the neighbor's Great Dane.

But for us, the true charmer of the facility is Tootsie, a tortoise that is a veritable sprinter as tortoises go. With luck, she'll live to be over a hundred years old.

With luck, Tootsie will be flirting with strangers for another ninety-six years.

Stalked on the Beach

Madison

It's not just any state park, no way. Hammonasset Beach State Beach not only boasts the longest stretch of publicly owned beach (3 miles worth, in fact) in the state, the place is also Connecticut's most popular state park and has landed numerous awards from a whole mess of publications.

It is also, we must point out, a hotbed of UFO activity.

Before you run to the cupboard for your alien repellent, in this case UFO stands for Unusual Flying Objects (which you are likely to see if you visit the park on a day when the weather is decent). The reason is simple: Hammonasset's sprawling 1,100 acres of beach, open fields, and hiking trails borders the tiny but unusually interesting Griswold Airport. This modest aerodrome is the home of a mighty fleet of about twelve privately owned aircraft. Seven of this dozen are tiny, fragile-looking ultralight aircraft, and the rest are single-engine airplanes.

Oh sure, it looks tranquil now, but keep your eyes on the sky. There are strange and wonderful flying machines in these parts.

If you take a stroll on the boardwalk lining part of the beach, don't be surprised to find yourself being shadowed by a small, low-flying (and unusually quiet) ultralight airplane that looks like the product of a boat mating with a kite. Other craft are often seen circling the park, including some classic light planes from the 1950s and earlier that are in excellent shape. Some of the smaller ultralights look as though they are moving barely faster than walking speed when they fly into the stiffer breezes off the bay and hover above you.

"You never really know what you might see out here," one park patron explains. "A lot of those things look like model airplanes that got out of hand. You'd never catch me in one, but they sure are fun to watch."

They Call It Art

Madison

One of the wonderful things about Connecticut is the quaint atmosphere of our small towns. Madison is no exception, and to meander down the Boston Post Road through the center of town is to recall a simpler, more traditional time. Except for all the modern art, that is.

Words like "bizarre" and "controversial" typically follow works of modern art like a trailer full of critics. To have such avant-garde works of outdoor sculpture displayed throughout a Colonial venue like downtown Madison is a bold move indeed—weird, even. But it shows that the sponsors of the "Madison Mile" as it is called are as interested in embracing the future as they are in preserving the past.

This exhibition tries to be as diverse as possible, mixing in more conventional works with some truly unusual and singular pieces that defy easy explanation or understanding.

"There are works that will challenge certain sensibilities," explains the guidebook to Madison's "Living Museum" of outdoor sculpture. This is certainly true. In fact, when we first encountered the exhibition (something we were certainly not expecting) and came across works such as Erwin Hauer's *Snowman* or Armand Saiia's *Spirit Gong* in proximity to the more traditional 315-year-old Deacon John Grave House, we thought aliens might have landed. To see the imaginations of artists from all over Connecticut, New England, and the world rendered in hard materials among more mundane items (like fire hydrants) is to see into a mind that is not bound by conventional ideas. Not surprisingly, this makes some folks uncomfortable. But such is the wonderful nature of art, especially art that is all over town so that residents interact with it on their daily errands. This exhibition is like a new car that's painted a wild, green-yellow color in a parking lot. You either like it or you don't, but it grabs your attention.

Contemporary art meets traditional New England.

The Madison Mile is divided into four sections with roughly forty pieces on display, and half of the exhibits are changed every six months. Outdoor art such as this makes a casual trip out to the shops much more entertaining—and makes this gutsy community stand out from the conventional definition of "downtown." These exhibits are part of the patronage of the Hollycroft Foundation, and for more information on current works on display contact William Bendig at (860) 767–2624.

A Shrine to a Floating Battery

Madison

Since Connecticut is so well stocked with history, it holds vast numbers of preserved dwellings that have been here for hundreds of years. A substantial number of these have been taken over by local historical societies, too, which fill them with period furniture and artifacts and also use them for office space and historical libraries.

The Madison Historical Society (203-245-4567) has done exactly this with the historic Allis-Bushnell house at 853 Boston Post Road. In this house you'll find great period items and furnishings that give you a glimpse into Colonial living. The house's most famous occupant was Cornelius Bushnell, famous founder of the Union Pacific Railroad. But as famous as that significant accomplishment made him, he is best known for helping make a reality one of the strangest craft ever to float. Ultimately this ship wasn't a huge success, but it did turn out to be a factor in the North's victory in the Civil War.

Bushnell was the financial backer and promoter for the *Monitor*, the strange flat warship designed by Swedish inventor John Ericsson that had a sea-level deck with a huge pillbox turret in the center. The craft was launched in early 1862 and later in the year fought a stalemate battle against the Confederate ironclad vessel *Virginia,* more commonly known by its original name, the *Merrimac.* The *Monitor* eventually sank off the North Carolina coast during a storm.

The Allis-Bushnell house has a veritable shrine to the famous ship in a building behind the house, which includes clippings, documents, photos, artwork, and a truly beautiful model of the innovative craft. So odd was the *Monitor*'s appearance that nicknames like "cheese box on a raft," "magic hat," and "floating battery" followed it wherever it sailed. The substantial wooden model lets you see the ship in three dimensions and, incidentally, was an oddity itself—for years nobody at the Madison Historical Society knew where the model came from or who constructed it. But excellent detective work by the society's Claire McKillip determined that the model was built in 1974 by the A. G. Hennings Company at the bequest of Phillip Platt, a past president of the society.

A mysterious model is mysterious no more.

Roadside Art, Part Trois

Marlborough

As if Hebron road art isn't enough: A few years ago, Violet Schwarz-mann had an inspiration driving down Marlborough's Route 66. A rock unearthed by utility workers would make a wonderful box turtle. And so Schwarzmann, who handles social services and the senior center in town, began organizing some teenagers to transform the rock into Tom the Turtle.

No one knows the origin of the need to paint perfectly adequate rocks, but it certainly adds to the panache of small burgs that might otherwise just be drive-throughs. A few residents expressed concern. One parent said the rock gives her child nightmares, but the support has been overwhelmingly in favor of the rock. So it stays, resting there by the road, watching over drivers, and peeking out from the snows come spring.

Say hello to Marlborough's largest turtle.

But Don't You Dare Pet It

Meriden

There's a legend that when hikers make it to the top of West Peak, they may run into an apparition in the shape of a black dog. The dog supposedly never approaches hikers, but hikers know how to communicate with the mangy beast.

The dog supposedly barks without making a sound and leaves no trace of its presence—no footprints, no nothing.

Hikers lucky enough to see the dog once can expect good fortune. The second dog sighting signals bad luck. The third time means death.

Unchained Objets d'Art

Middlefield

You're motoring along Meriden Road in Middlefield, and you say to yourself, "Gee, it's not every day you see an 8-foot lawn giraffe looming over a 1959 two-tone Ford Galaxie."

You're right. Even the people who pass Jimmy D's Antiques Plus at 228 Middlefield Road (860–343–8434) every day on their way to Middletown don't typically see these two items next to each other, because the inanimate inhabitants of this sizable emporium tend to move around a lot.

CASH PAID FOR UNWANTED ITEMS, reads the sign, and this is a kingdom for unwanted and unloved possessions that you must see to appreciate. Stroll out back and you will walk down a well-worn trail that meanders through canyons of either treasures or trash, depending on your point of view.

To your right is a classic Coke machine, leaning at an odd angle but sporting a sign that says it works perfectly and it costs $750. To your left, a collection of dodgem cars, ten in number, look a bit wild out in the open without their customary enclosed carnival arena to protect them. A

Jeep pickup looks forlornly at a strange wooden cowboy, who ignores the inert vehicle and seems to have his eye on yet another Ford Galaxie, this one a 1962 model. Through it all are lawn ornaments, scooters, and the occasional garden tiller with an engine that has been picked over by that omnipresent scavenger, the parts-seeking junkyard buzzard.

Large tents house all kinds of furniture, some of it quite desirable. It's easy to get lost in all these artifacts, which makes it kind of a neat place—in an "Island of Misfit Belongings" sort of way.

Won't You Come Home, George Bailey?
Middletown

Movie director Frank Capra bought a self-published short story in the mid-1940s for $10,000. He was just back from serving in the Office of War Information, where his *Why We Fight* films had become classics. He wanted something calmer, something that reassured the American public that despite all that was happening, all was right with the world.

The short story would be his first plunge back into moviemaking since his stint with the military. The same was true of his star, Jimmy Stewart, who had left Hollywood to serve with distinction in the Air Force, leading 1,000 plane strikes against Germany. Capra was sure about his star, but he compiled a list of twenty-two actors to play one of the story's supporting roles, Uncle Billy. He found Thomas Mitchell, an actor who'd become famous for portraying Jesus in Cecil B. DeMille's 1927 *King of Kings*—to play a drunk. And the cast for *It's a Wonderful Life,* the film that plays on an endless loop around the holidays, was finally complete.

Production notes, correspondence between Capra and his troupe, letters from fans around the world—and from librarians angry that Capra had portrayed Mary, played by Donna Reed, as a rather homely and hapless librarian—Capra kept them all. When he needed a place to store his papers, mementos, and other treasures, the Sicilian immigrant and former pipe inspector left them to the Wesleyan Cinema Archives in 1981. In 1986 Jeanine Basinger, Wesleyan University Corwin-Fuller professor of film studies and archives curator, wrote *The It's a Wonderful Life Book*.

Capra died in 1991. Critics originally strafed his film, and some continue to do so for its open-eyed wonder and the basic decency of the small-town characters—even "the richest and meanest man in the county," Henry F. Potter, played by a grousing Lionel Barrymore.

The archives are open to "scholars, students, and other researchers working on bona fide topics." If you fall into any of those categories, call the archives at (860) 685–3396.

A City For Kids

Middletown

Before we launch into this wild gigantic playscape that earned mention in this book from the size of its sign alone, we should note something unusual right off the bat: When was the last time you went to an attraction where the price of admission for both kids and adults was the same?

At the KidCity Museum at 119 Washington Street in Middletown (860–347–0495, www.kidcitymuseum.com), the only way you get in at a special rate is if you're less than twelve months of age. This policy is appropriate, because in some ways the kids are the adults in this city. They get to encounter a variety of rooms including a scaled-down Main Street that allows them to go grocery shopping, and therefore get a glimpse of the adult world years before they will have to deal with the real thing on a daily basis (and all the fun is taken out of it).

There's tons more, of course, including a musical planet, a farm, a ship and other great mini-venues for kids to exercise their imaginations far away from the world of TV and video games.

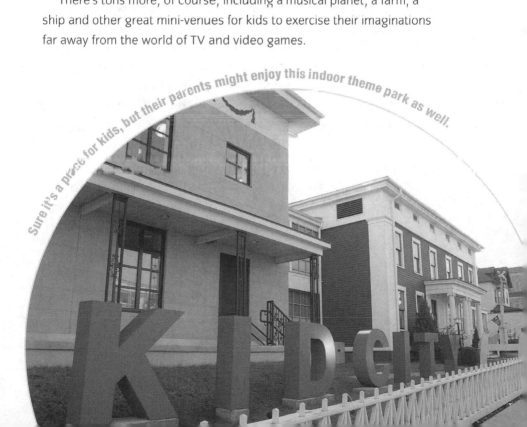

Sure it's a price for kids, but their parents might enjoy this indoor theme park as well.

KidCity is a volunteer-run nonprofit, the creation of founder Jennifer Alexander and a lot of fine folks who remember what being a kid is all about. The main building itself has an enchanting history, for it started life as the convent for the St. Sebastian Church and used to reside more than a football field's distance away from its present location.

Now an addition has been added and there's enough space for a lot of young 'uns to explore and act out many a fantasy. This is their city, to be sure, but their parents will appreciate the place, too. The sound of so many kids having fun is pretty much worth the price of admission alone.

Hashing Out Haute Cuisine
Middletown

The exterior of the building has a certain run-down quality that can only be found on diners that have been around for a long, long time. It stands out all the more because it seems to occupy its own special kingdom at the north end of Main Street in Middletown. In fact, these days the old restaurant almost looks out of place, considering how the downtown area is starting to look more upscale all the time.

But there is something quite wonderfully unexpected about O'Rourke's Diner (860–346–6101) in that it is not just another blue plate special kind of a joint. The food here is anything but ordinary—and nothing short of stunning. Specializing in breakfast and lunch (with a private dinner once a month or so), this diner has been dubbed one of the finest places to eat in the state over and over again by a broad variety of publications and has even been praised in *Gourmet* magazine.

"I think we've been written up in just about every magazine there is," muses owner and chef Brian O'Rourke.

What the heck is going on here? Aren't weatherbeaten old diners mostly about bad coffee and excessively poached eggs, topped with a hollandaise from hell straight out of a jar?

"We do our own bread, soups, sauces—everything is from scratch," explains O'Rourke. "Our weekend breakfast menu has more than a hundred items on it. We have some fabulous French toast specials every week, and too many other things to mention."

You can never judge anything solely by appearance. There's a pearl in this Middletown oyster that looks like an overgrown Airstream trailer with too many miles on it. "Words can't do anything," states O'Rourke. "You have to see the operation to believe it."

Just another greasy spoon, right? No way. The food in this modest diner will literally blow your culinary socks off.

Don't Be a Stranger
Portland

It's a friendly little admonition: COME ON OVER painted in large letters on a reinforced concrete wall in Portland, just above the Connecticut River. Any one looking over the river from Middletown can see it.

The original sentiment was placed there by John C. Barry, owner of the old Strong & Hale (great name, yes?) Lumber Yard. In 1925, he build a 10-foot-by-132-foot concrete retaining wall and then, maybe because the wall looked too drab, or maybe because he had a bit of whimsy to him, he painted it red and then added the large, white block letters, COME ON OVER.

It was one of those sweet, small-town things that people like to comment on, but the wall started to deteriorate, and so in the late '90s, a couple of citizens, including a grandson of Barry's, volunteered to

rebuild the wall. The local Exchange Club got involved and, within two weeks, the wall was up and painted. It took a dozen Exchange Club members roughly five work sessions to finish. People say it's just fine—although there's no word on how many people cross the river just because the sign tells them to.

Who could resist such a friendly invite?

Big Roadside Wienie

Portland

Andrea Spaulding wanted a restaurant; instead, her husband got her a 16-foot trailer rebuilt to look like a hot dog in a bun with all the fixings (except chili, which would be a tough mold on the giant wienie).

If he thought a huge Fiberglass wienie would get the restaurant business—a tough one, even on a good day—out of her system, he thought wrong. That was twenty-one years ago.

Customers swear by the hot dogs—and so does she. "I still eat them," says Andrea Spaulding, patting her stomach; "I would be a size 2, otherwise. I wish I knew how many we sold each year."

Husband Al has also restored a yellow taxi, which they intend to use to pull the hot dog to fairgrounds and the like in season. Look for the big hot dog with fixings on the south side of Route 66 in Portland, just west of Main Street. If you're lucky, Al will have parked his completely restored 1972 Checker Special cab right next to it. The restaurant, like so many Connecticut establishments, is seasonal and generally stays open from April to November.

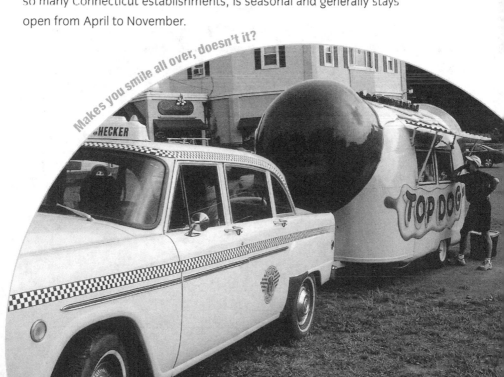

Makes you smile all over, doesn't it?

GOD'S BELLYACHES

For as long as anyone can remember, the caves in and around Moodus have emitted some very strange noises, indeed. Some say they sound like a train. Others say they sound more like distant thunder. (We're inclined to say they're somewhere between the two. Why pick sides?)

So what's up in Moodus?

The Wangunk Indians lived in what is now the Moodus area when the first European settlers came through in 1670 or thereabouts. The Wangunks were used to the noises and warned their new neighbors about them. They treated the noises as one might a mark on the calendar: When the noises started up, the Wangunks held a tribal meeting. It was like a subterranean pager. In fact, the name of the town, which the Europeans adopted, was originally Machemoodus, or "place of noises." Not everyone heard the sounds, and sometimes the ground would be quiet for years.

Explanations for the noises ranged from the god Manitou rolling over in his sleep to that same god suffering from a stomachache to wind shooting through the Moodus caves. Later, some speculators suggested earthquakes, but the earth didn't quake when the noises could be heard, so that idea was dismissed.

That is the explanation, however, that scientists eventually settled on: The Moodus noises are caused by small earthquakes not detectable by anything but machines. We suggest you decide the cause for yourself. Personally, we like god's tummyaches better. The noises are particularly pronounced at Mt. Tom, near the confluence of the Salmon and Moodus Rivers.

They Called It Horsepower

Rocky Hill

There's nothing quite like sitting on the bank of one of Connecticut's amazing rivers and watching things evolve. We've spent years doing it, in fact—especially keeping an eye on the mighty Connecticut River, which has been such an important source of transportation for all kinds of living creatures. In this substantial body of water, we've seen all kinds of aquatic creatures adapt over time to their surroundings, typically finding better, more efficient ways to live on the river.

The Rocky Hill–Glastonbury Ferry is one of these creatures, oddly enough. This modest little shipping concern has been carrying passengers and other items across the river for so long, it has garnered the unusual distinction of being the oldest continually operating ferry in these United States. If you're taking Route 160 and want to travel from Rocky Hill to Glastonbury (or vice versa) it's still the only way to cross the river.

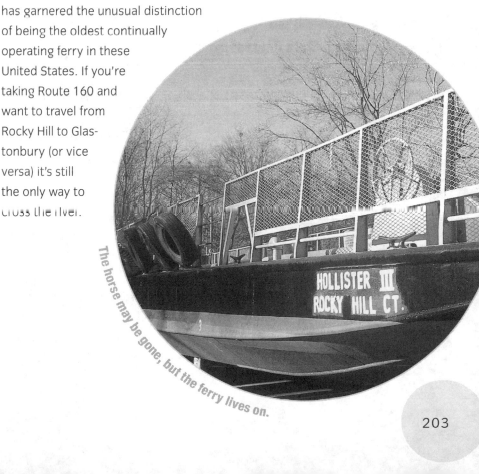

The horse may be gone, but the ferry lives on.

What's really wild about this particular aquatic "creature" is that while the journey across the river hasn't changed much, the ferry itself has evolved quite a bit. Back in 1655 the ferry was basically just a log raft pushed along by poles. This was eventually replaced with a strange craft that was powered by a horse on a treadmill, which is as novel a way to power a boat as you'll ever come across. It must have been a particularly strange way to make a living if you were the horse—used to using its legs to get somewhere and yet stuck on that danged boat no matter how hard it worked. In the 1870s steam power replaced the pony, and these days a diesel-powered tug tows the Hollister III—a large, flat barge that can hold three cars—from shore to shore. Just $3.00 gets you across the river in about four minutes.

Our Official State Depression
Rocky Hill

The state of Connecticut has a boatload of symbols to tell the world who the heck we are. There is of course the State Song ("Yankee Doodle"), State Bird (American robin), State Shellfish (Eastern oyster), and even a State Motto ("He who transplanted still sustains"). We have no idea what that last bit means exactly, but there you are.

But, hey, who cares about all this pretentious pomp? A state is truly measured by the quality and character of its State Fossil. And in Connecticut we have a doozy—a huge, menacing footprint of a meat-eating dinosaur that roamed the state well before the Lady Huskies began their first basketball practice.

It all started when construction worker Edward McCarthy unearthed a chunk of sandstone with his bulldozer back in 1966. He was working on the land for a new state building at 400 West Street in Rocky Hill and in the process discovered a veritable treasure trove of dinosaur foot-

Extinction may not have been such a bad thing.

prints that were made during the Jurassic period, about 200 million years ago.

Once this find was discovered, plans changed abruptly. The state knew it had something more important at this site than a prospective office. Experts were called in, the tracks were carefully preserved, and State Troopers kept watch to discourage renegade paleontologists/souvenir hunters. Dinosaur State Park (860–529–8423, www.dinosaurstatepark.org) was opened officially in 1968, and a huge geodesic dome now protects the prints and houses a host of very cool exhibits.

As for the biggest (and most menacing) prints themselves, they're called Eubrontes. No, that's not the dinosaur that made them, for since it's often impossible to be sure what species made footprints (and there aren't any bones left in the area), the prints themselves are given a name. But experts agree that the rascal that left his three-toed marks in the mud was most likely closely related to *Dilophosaurus,* a nasty-looking beastie who reached a length of more than 20 feet and whose bones have been found in Arizona.

But it's the fossilized prints, not ol' Dilo (as his friends called him), that the state has recognized. Thus we have a depression we can be proud of here in this land of Jurassic commuters.

Mermaids Asleep with the Fishes
Salem

Fishers at Gardner Lake swear they hear mermaids playing piano from far, far away. Well, maybe they don't hear it from that far away. In fact, the sound seems to come from directly below, underwater in the 487-acre lake.

In 1895, a Salem family wanted to move their two-story house across Gardner Lake, so they waited until the water froze and hired eighteen horses to pull it across by skids. Unfortunately, things went awry, a warm rain helped melt the ice during the process, and the next morning, the house was sinking. In rather short order, it slipped beneath the surface and sank in 30 feet of water—lock, stock, and family piano.

Imagine the distress of all concerned. It was a total loss—except for area anglers who swear by the lake's prize bass, perch, and pickerel. Irony of ironies, Gardner Lake is a popular spot particularly for winter ice fishing and multiple fishing tournaments through the years. The house is just about destroyed, rotted away beneath the water, but the fish live on. As do the mermaids. Where else can you get a fish and a melody, all in one stop?

The Truck as Community Calendar
Wallingford

Since ancient times—going back way, way before Connecticut Governor Lowell Weicker's administration—man has used a variety of devices to track the inevitable, inexorable change of the seasons. From rocks carefully arranged to point to the various celestial turning points (like the autumnal equinox) to the amazing accuracy of the hardware store freebie calendar, the human species has successfully come up with clever ways to tell us it's cold outside.

But all these great advances pale in comparison with the Truck That Tells Time. This well-worn farm vehicle is decorated to suit the season, and the folks who pass by the Beaumont Farm on East Center Street have been admiring the aged vehicle for, oh, well, the farm has been in the family since 1899, but the truck has actually been famous for a considerably shorter period of time.

A seasonal planter loved by the community.

The vehicle in question is a 1929 Chevrolet flatbed, which was built in combination with the remains of another ancient Chevrolet flatbed. When Billy Beaumont decided in the spring of 2001 to put the truck on the corner where people could see it he had no idea what he had wrought. "I had the truck and I was looking at it, and it looked so terrible that I asked myself, *What in the world am I gonna do with this thing?*" he explains. "I decided I might as well just make a big flower planter out of it."

Billy and Company spruced the truck up, filled the back with dirt, and put it on the corner of the farm right across from a stoplight on Center Street. "We planted it last spring, and it's been full of flowers ever since, growing right out of the back of the truck," says Billy.

One thing led to another and the Beaumonts started decorating the truck with a seasonal theme (pumpkins around Halloween, Santa driving for Christmas, etc.). The response was kind of amazing. "People are coming in here all the time talking about it," he laughs. "Even a local hot rod association came by and wanted to know if we had another one, because they wanted to put one in their front yard. The truck has been on the news programs, in newspapers, you name it. People really love to see what we'll do with it next."

By the way, you can tell when Christmas is getting near; the truck gradually gets so full of Santa's loot it's almost buried.

Where the Pay Is Only Slightly Worse Than the Prestige
Wethersfield

Say you're of a certain age, bored, and looking for a way to revive an interest in history—but mostly, you're bored. If you're Richard B. Lasher, you appoint yourself honorary mayor of Griswoldville—an honest-to-goodness former town that got swallowed up by the current-day Wethersfield, site of the book *Witch of Blackbird Pond*. And you let it be known that you ran on the Mugwump ticket, an honest-to-good-ness former political party.

Only you make both Griswoldville and the Mugwump ticket your own, with campaign slogans like "I straddle the fence on every issue; thusly, my mug is on one side of the fence, and my wump is on the other side; and I'm for my friends!"

You even circulate campaign posters with your face superimposed on the body of a buff male model and add more slogans: "When Did My Wild Oats Turn Into Shredded Wheat?" "Over the Hill & On a Roll," and "Maybe. And That's Final."

And if people complain? Or the little white wagon pulls up out front? Blame your campaign advisers, the stouthearted burghers of Gris-woldville. In a recent election, the good mayor says he squeaked by with six vote—the same number of names his campaign managers took off the stones of a local cemetery. His Honorary lives on—of course—Griswold Road. But don't bother him. Imaginary affairs of state keep him plenty busy.

SOUTHEAST

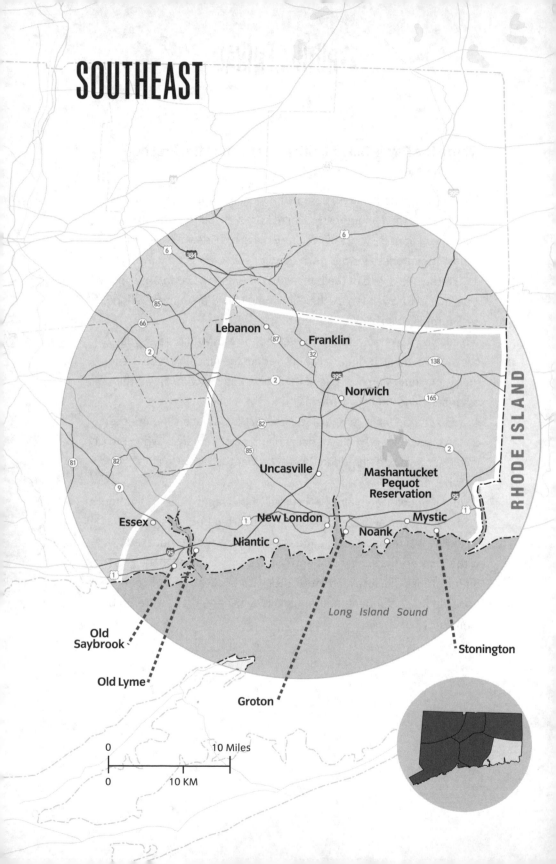

Lebanon

Franklin

Norwich

Uncasville

Mashantucket
Pequot
Reservation

Essex

New London

Mystic

Niantic

Noank

Long Island Sound

RHODE ISLAND

Old
Saybrook

Old Lyme

Groton

Stonington

0   10 Miles

0   10 KM

SOUTHEAST

A Very Short Ride Indeed
Essex

Few things are as bracing as an ocean voyage, although a river voyage can come pretty close, provided the river is big enough. The feel of the spray, the sway of your vessel under the power of the swells, the endless horizon; all these sensations (and many more) combine to lift the spirit and invigorate the soul.

Well, if the ferry isn't running, you can always swim for it.

The question is, how long does a voyage have to be to qualify? Can you consider yourself a seasoned mariner if your aquatic expedition lasts only for a minute—including loading and unloading? What if the "crossing" actually only covers a distance you could throw a rock—and a fair-sized one at that?

The journey regularly undertaken by the Essex Island Marina Ferry may be the shortest ferry voyage in the United States. It's certainly the shortest in Connecticut, as it takes you from the foot of Ferry Street on mainland Essex to the Island Marina (860–767–1267, http://essexisland marina.com), which occupies a privately owned island on the Connecticut River. The ferry, by the way, is actually a water taxi rather than the type of auto ferry most of us are used to. In fact, if you try to drive your car onto it, you will sink the ferry, douse your auto, and fall out of favor with the locals.

But aside from the ferry being limited to passengers, it has numerous advantages. The duration of the journey means that provisions are not necessary, people rarely get seasick, and cases of piracy and scurvy are practically unheard of. Sometimes the shortest trips *are* the best.

Maybe you didn't know it (and maybe you didn't care) but Oxoboxo Lake in New London County is a palindrome, or a word that's spelled the same backward and forward, like pop or ma'am. Neat, huh?

SO YOU LIKED THE MOVIE *SIDEWAYS*? THEN YOU'LL LOVE CONNECTICUT.

Ben Franklin might have said, "Beer is living proof that God loves us and wants us to be happy." Galileo is supposed to have said "Wine is sunlight held together by water." He was from Tuscany, and most likely he knew what he was talking about.

Connecticut is a long way from Tuscany, but only geographically. Residents living anywhere in the state are no more than forty-five minutes from a vineyard. The rocky soil and the state's microclimates make the Nutmeg State an ideal incubator for lovely grapes.

Wine tastings dot the warmer months. Places like Stonington Vineyards rely on people coming to their picture-pretty sloping hills to sample the wares. Stonington, which has been in business since the late '80s, sells 80 percent of its wine from the vineyard retail room. There and elsewhere, you can enjoy tastings, tours, and seasonal gatherings. Go ahead. Wine isn't just for high-class folks. We can drink it, too!

For more information on some of Connecticut's vineyards, visit www.ctwine.com.

A Mock Turtle like No Other
Essex

The Revolutionary War certainly had no shortage of heroes, and Connecticut is filled with tales of bold battles and courageous exploits. In addition to brave deeds, a great deal of innovative thinking also took place here during the Revolution. In one case it meant creating an entirely new form of warfare. Thanks to a couple of dedicated craftsmen, one of the weirdest contraptions ever created has been reborn for new generations to gaze upon and ask, "What the hell is that?"

The "that" is the *Turtle,* originally built in Saybrook around 1775 by David and Ezra Bushnell. Considered by many to be the world's first operational submarine, this roughly 8-foot-tall craft resembled an enormous tick sitting upright or an equally huge walnut—or, perhaps, a turtle. This submersible housed one operator and was designed to cruise underneath British ships and attach a mine to the hull. Then this strangely housed intruder would light the waterproof fuse and furiously hand-crank the propulsion propeller to escape. After extensive testing in the Connecticut River, the *Turtle* brought submarine technology to war in New York Harbor, although it was never able to successfully attach a mine to a ship.

But the curious device impressed all who saw it (including, it is said, some inventor-type named Ben Franklin) and was without a doubt the father of undersea warfare, at least in theory. And thanks to the incredible efforts of Joseph Leary and Frederick Friesé in 1976, the Connecticut River Museum at 67 Main Street in Essex (860–767–8269, www .ctrivermuseum.org) has the world's only full-scale, functional *Turtle* model on display. It's a very weird vessel, to be sure, but you can't help but admire the incredible ingenuity that went into the design all those years ago—or the bravery of the poor soul inside, furiously cranking to safety.

NOT YOUR EVERYDAY TOWN GROUNDHOG

For as long as anyone cares to remember, Essex has celebrated Groundhog Day with a parade. The heart of this parade, of course, is a nearly-8-foot-tall, 200-pound foam-and-fiberglass weather-guesser whose name is Essex Ed.

No, he's not Punxsutawney Phil, the better-known Pennsylvania prognosticator, but we love him. Unlike that real-life rodent, sometimes he wears interesting costumes (firefighter, Dutch explorer Adriaen Block, and once Professor Hill, the conman in the musical *The Music Man*). Originally Essex Ed was born to break the boredom of New England's longest month (at least it seems that way), and since then things have gotten a little louder. Local inns in this charming river town fill up on Groundhog Day weekend. Ed's annual trip down Main Street is generally heralded by a few hundred spectators banging pots and pans. The banging, of course, is meant to wake him up so that he can end winter already and move Connecticut into an early spring. Sometimes it works.

Wanna see Essex Ed? Mark your Groundhog Day calendar!

Smile When You Park Here, Pardner
Franklin

You got your horse, and he needs some tack. Maybe a new saddle blanket is in order. Dang, you wouldn't mind getting yourself a new hat while you're at it and a belt buckle for LouAnn.

The thing is, you want to go some place . . . western. You love Connecticut, but you would love it if we had a taste of the Old West, even if just for a little while.

Behold the Little B Barn at 43 Manning Road in Franklin (860–642–6901, www.littlebarntack.com). Once you drive your pickup into the parking lot, you'll hear the likes of George Strait and Willie Nelson over the loudspeakers. There's an entire Western town in front of you, including a livery stable, marshal's office, jail, bank, undertaker's, blacksmith shop, and what we think is a brothel (but don't tell the law about that part). There are even a few carved residents to give the scene additional atmosphere.

It's all a facade of course, but a dang good one. The store is well stocked with all manner of equestrian needs, whether you ride Western or English style. Shoot, there's lots of stuff here even if you don't ride but just like horses (or need a gift for someone who does). No other tack shop we've visited has the entertaining ambience of the Little B; that in itself makes it worth the ride.

Gungywamps of the Gods?
Groton

You may not have heard of Gungywamp, but it is ours and ours alone. Ultimately, what does this mean? Well, for one thing, it means that Connecticut will not be overshadowed by the likes of Stonehenge and Easter Island when it comes to archeological mysteries.

Gungywamp is the name given to a scenically beautiful part of the state that encompasses about twenty acres of land near Groton, which coincidentally has some unusual stone sites on it. Access is limited because the land is privately owned (half belongs to the YMCA). Exactly what this collection of pointed stone remains and strange chambers is (or was) is a mystery. And as with any other type of mystery, there's the factual side: Who originally built the site? What was the significance of the construction of some of the cavelike chambers that are found there?

Then there's the wild stuff, like tales of strange magnetic fields and a cliff that supposedly makes people feel really depressed.

So what we have at the Gungywamp site is either some rather intriguing lithic remains and chambers or, depending on who you talk to, some sort of weird supernatural portal.

We talked primarily with Paulette Buchanon, who in addition to being a history professor at Eastern Connecticut State University is also the corresponding secretary and tour guide for the Gungywamp Society (www.gungywamp.com). Her society is dedicated to the scholarly exploration of the site, and she is Gungywamp's Agent Scully (of X-Files fame) in that she prefers science to speculation.

"We have archeological proof that the area was inhabited by settlers in the Colonial era," she says. "There's all kinds of weird theories about the site, but we think it was just an ancient settlement that was occupied by different settlers over time. But," she adds, "there is one sub-chamber that is kind of strange. If you're in the chamber at the right time of day, the sun comes through an opening and a beam of light works its way across the wall. Eventually this beam hits a particular rock, and it illuminates part of the sub-chamber. It's really kind of weird, and we have no idea who built it."

Strange and interesting, this Gungywamp. The society will give you an excellent tour of the area for $5.00, and you are free to feel either enlightened or depressed, depending on your point of view.

The Peroxide Torpedo Hauler
Groton

Quick! What common household item once appeared to hold the key to the submersible longevity of the modern submarine? No, it's not baking soda. I know those little baking soda–powered bathtub submarines are cool, but this was an actual sub that carried people and torpedoes and such.

The household substance we're talking about is hydrogen peroxide, and the submarine that used this wonderful healer of cuts and maker of many a blond tress was the USS *X-1*. This amazing underwater vessel had a truly revolutionary powerplant that allowed, for the first time, a submarine to stay submerged under power for long periods of time without surfacing to run conventional diesel engines and recharge the batteries. It would have formed the basis for our modern attack submarines if not for one piddling little detail: nuclear power. Dang those atoms! And to think my ancestors traded heavily in hydrogen peroxide futures!

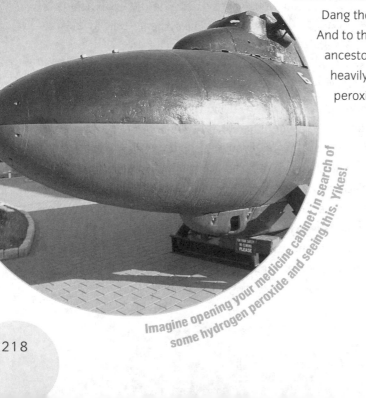

Imagine opening your medicine cabinet in search of some hydrogen peroxide and seeing this. Yikes!

About the same time that the Navy was developing the amazing nuclear-powered *Nautilus*, the novel propulsion system residing in the *X-1*'s compact, maneuverable hull was also being tested. Essentially, a closed-loop hydrogen peroxide system provided the necessary air to run a diesel engine underwater, which had not previously been possible. The better efficiency and reliability of nuclear power, however, rendered the *X-1*'s peroxide system obsolete. Such systems are still used by other navies around the world, however.

Since, like the *Nautilus*, the *X-1* ushered in a new era of lengthy submarine submersion, it is totally appropriate that this sub sits right next to where the mighty *Nautilus* is moored at the Submarine Force Museum in Groton (800–343–0079, www.uss.nautilus.org). The little underachiever often gets overlooked, but once you see it and recognize its important contribution to submarine development, you'll never look at a bottle of hydrogen peroxide the same way again. You can find it at 1 Crystal Lake Road.

Will the Real Nautilus Please Surface?

Groton

It all started when a scientist (whose name eludes us) decided to name a fairly ancient and unusual species of aquatic life the nautilus. It's a wild-looking little beastie, and it's safe to say that most people have never actually seen one in the flesh.

It's also safe to say that most people in Connecticut are familiar with the name. After all, our state is home to one of the most significant submarines ever built—the first nuclear-powered vessel ever to cruise beneath the waves. The USS *Nautilus* was also the first to reach the North Pole, and it set countless other records before being decommissioned in 1980 after steaming nearly 500,000 miles during its career.

The name comes from another submarine called *Nautilus*, also powered by nuclear energy. Only this submarine never actually got wet or raised its periscope or even performed a crash dive. This submarine was the invention of Jules Verne and appeared on the literary scene all the way back in 1850. In *20,000 Leagues Under the Sea* Verne predicted the invention of the nuclear-powered underwater vessel more than one hundred years before the real thing came to pass in 1954.

But Verne wasn't the first to use the name. Robert Fulton christened his submersible invention the *Nautilus* around 1800. Even though Fulton's invention worked, he couldn't get anyone in the armed services interested in it.

So while it's not surprising that the U.S. Navy chose to honor Verne (and Fulton, too, we wager) by choosing that name for its nuclear sub, what is surprising is that nearly half a dozen other ships had been named *Nautilus* before the nuclear version arrived.

Can you imagine that? How can a ship that's not a nuclear submarine dare to call itself *Nautilus*, anyway? Fulton gets a pass here, because sci-fi writers hadn't yet dreamed of nuclear power when he built his invention. And he *was* the first to label a submarine with the name, after all.

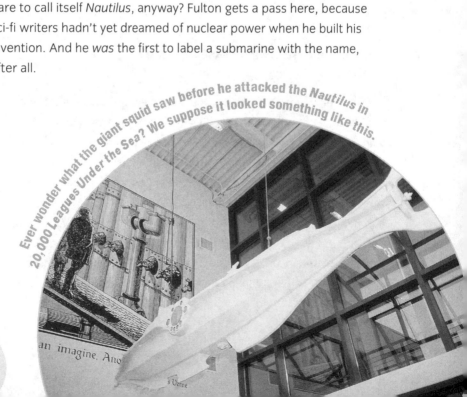

Ever wonder what the giant squid saw before he attacked the *Nautilus* in *20,000 Leagues Under the Sea*? We suppose it looked something like this.

But as far as we're concerned, there's really been only three *Nautilus*es, and we're happy to report that Connecticut has the two most famous. One is moored in the channel outside the Submarine Force Museum in Groton (800–343–0079, www.uss.nautilus.org), and the other is in the foyer of that same museum, which is located at 1 Crystal Lake Road. It's a beautiful model of Verne's *Nautilus* based on the one in the 1954 Disney film, masterfully constructed in 1986 (when the museum opened) by David Bishop.

War-Time Spin, Circa 1781

Groton

On September 6, 1781, roughly 800 British troops stormed Fort Griswold in Groton, which was defended by 165 ragtag volunteers led by Colonel William Ledyard. The bloodbath lasted forty minutes, until Ledyard was stabbed. Local history says he was stabbed as he was surrendering his sword to a British officer. The officer is supposed to have cried to Ledyard, "Who commands this fort?" And Ledyard was said to have replied, "I did, sir, but you do now," and then handed him his sword, with which the British officer ran Ledyard through.

It was a good story to tell among Connecticut volunteers—roughly 30 percent of whom sympathized with the British crown. A gallant leader. A lost cause. An ugly killing.

But it may have just been that, a good story. From the tears in the shirt and waistcoat he was wearing the day he died—those articles of clothing now the property of the Connecticut Historical Society—it would appear that he was, in fact, fighting to the death. And depositions taken by survivors of the battle reveal nothing about a death-at-surrender. Those stories only grew over time when survivors of the battle gave statements to collect pensions, sometimes fifty years later.

That won't change the plaques and the murals at Fort Griswold, now a state park, though. As one state worker at the fort says, "We'll probably just stick to our original story."

The fort, in remarkable condition, all things considered, is at 57 Fort Street in Groton. Call (860) 445–1729 for more information.

We may never know the mystery of Fort Griswold.

George Washington's Horse Might Have Slept Here. Sort Of.

Lebanon

Oh, the sticky wicket of trying to prove the movements of Our First President. If George Washington didn't record a stop in his diary (not much attended to during the war years) or in his detailed financial records, then proving a stay (or lunch or tea) is particularly difficult.

Nevertheless, we like this story, and we're sticking to it: In September 1780, George Washington passed through Hartford and stayed at the home of the Wadsworth family, whose home was where the Wadsworth Atheneum stands now on Main Street.

While he stayed there, Washington's beloved horse, Nelson (the white charger seen so often in historical prints) was quartered at the family stables. In early 1800s, a fire raced through Hartford, and the stables were torn down to form a fire break. Some of those timbers, however, might have been used to rebuild the family's new stable in an ornate, Palladian style. Few pieces of wood were wasted, although the Wadsworth family certainly had the means to purchase new wood for their stable.

George Washington's horse may have slept here (twice removed).

Stay with us. It gets more interesting. In the mid-1950s, the probably historic stables were to be torn down, but the Connecticut Daughters of the American Revolution raised funds to buy the structure, take it apart, and reassemble it on the town green of Lebanon, a historic burg about 30 miles away.

Whether or not Nelson actually stayed in the original stable, a corner stall in the Lebanon structure has on its door a picture of the charger and a small name plate emblazoned NELSON. The stables are undergoing renovation to make the building presentable for community activities.

A Different Kind of Miracle Mile

Lebanon

What could be more New England-y than a white church steeple presiding over a town green? How about a white church steeple and a town green lined with historical houses and buildings?

Lebanon's green has it all. The French Cavalry drilled here. It's one of New England's largest greens. And it includes the War Office, once the store of a former governor, where colonists planned the defense of their land. Nearby is the home of that former governor, Jonathan Trumbull, who lead the state during the Revolutionary War. There's also the fancy, Palladian-style Wadsworth Stable, which was moved from Hartford in 1954, and said to have one time been a resting place for the horses of both George Washington and General Jean Baptiste Rochambeau, leader of the French army. So if Washington didn't sleep in the stable, at least his horse did. And here in New England, that means something.

And there is, of course, the quintessential white church, the First Congregational Church of Lebanon, from the early 1700s—the location of which spawned such heated discussions that the site of the building had to be decided by the state's General Assembly. (The present-day brick building was built in the early 1800s, according to designs by Trumbull. Here in Connecticut, the early 1800s qualifies as "new.")

The church and other historic sites are open to the public. For more information, visit www.lebanoncthistsoc.org. In all, there is more than a town-green-full of history here, and the sites are all within walking distance. You can walk the green via a nice 1.5 mile path—with benches. You'll find the green at the junction of Routes 87 and 289 in Lebanon.

Wagering on a Museum
Mashantucket

It's amazing how a person, or a people's, fortunes can change in a fairly short period of time. The Mashantucket Pequots (like just about every other group of Native Americans) have seen their share of poverty and despair. War with colonists and rival tribes decimated their ranks, and they gradually lost their land as the members of the tribe became scattered.

But in the 1970s tribal members started returning to their small reservation; in the 1980s they were granted formal recognition by the United States and a sizable portion of their land was returned to them. Economic activity followed and culminated with the building of the enormous Foxwoods casino in 1992.

Usually casinos merely enrich a few individuals or corporations; rarely do they enrich the culture of a nation. But the Mashantucket Pequots decided not only to use their newfound economic power to help record their history but also to invest in a rather spectacular museum and share their cultural development with the world.

Thankfully for all of us, they didn't do the Mashantucket Pequot Museum and Research Center halfway, either. At a cost approaching $200 million, this is an incredible facility, which is located at 110 Pequot

Trail (800–411–9671, www.pequotmuseum.org), and has everything from a simulated glacial crevasse (that creaks like you're about to plunge into the abyss) to re-created Pequot villages and forts. Every square foot of the facility uses the latest in audiovisual technology to make a visit something that will impress even the most well-traveled museum hound. Icing on the cake? A 185-foot stone and glass tower from which you can view the region.

Don't Just Rent the Movie; Eat the Pizza
Mystic

Los Angeles–based screenwriter Amy Jones summered in the Mystic area and came to love the Mystic Pizza, a local eatery established in 1973 by the Zelepos family. It was nothing extremely fancy, but the customers loved their little "slice of heaven," and so did Jones.

She wrote *Mystic Pizza* and set the bulk of the action around the factional-fictional restaurant and the exploits of its waitstaff, including a young and coltish Julia Roberts. Released in 1988, the picture pulled scads more tourists to the tiny corner restaurant. (While much of the movie was shot on location, the interior shots of the restaurant were actually a set, and the exteriors were a building in Stonington Borough. The original Mystic Pizza was too small and too dark for filming, and the owners couldn't see closing for months to allow the shooting.)

Within a few years the restaurant had expanded to the space next door, and in 1991 Mystic Pizza II opened in nextdoor North Stonington. It wasn't just the movie buzz that got people to visit; the pizza is that good. Now you can buy Mystic Pizza frozen, in your neighborhood grocery freezer. And then, enjoy the T-shirt made famous by Julia Roberts, pre-famous.

For more information, call the restaurant at (860) 536–3700 and 536–3737.

How Do They Do That?

Mystic

On the other end of Main Street from the popular Mystic Pizza is the country's oldest bascule drawbridge, which opens and lowers to allow boat traffic to cruise up the Mystic River. In summer months it opens hourly, and foot and vehicle traffic know to hurry off the bridge when the alarm sounds.

The bridge operates something like one of those plastic birds that dip into water. Huge weights on the Groton side of the river lower, and that swings the drawbridge into the air. When the bridge is fully opened, boats with tall masts (like the sailboats so popular in the area) can pass by.

Although we didn't find them, rumor is that there are people who are enthralled with the action of the bridge and will stand for hours recording it on videocamera. We're not sure we're *that* enthralled, but watching the boats go by is really the perfect cap to a visit to this New England seafaring village.

A Dry, Warm Trip to the Abyss

Mystic

You're standing on the deck of a mighty research vessel; the sound of diesel generators fills your ears, accompanied by the commands of crew members as they prepare the deep-sea submersible *Turtle* for a dive to the ocean's icy depths.

But there's something weird going on here. Even though you're way out at sea, you're in no danger of losing your lunch or falling overboard when the ship hits an unexpected swell. Better yet, while the water beneath you may contain eerie creatures of the deep, the odds that you will be attacked by a giant squid and dragged into the depths are very small indeed. These are, of course, welcome things—but how is it possible to be in such an adventurous setting and yet be spared the hazards of a potentially dangerous expedition?

The ship that seems so steady on the surface of what we know is a dynamic ocean is the *Discovery,* and it's actually a replica of a very famous research vessel that has traveled the world performing deep-sea exploration. Walking onto this stationary vessel marks the start of something unique in all the world: a dry, comfortable trip into the inkiest of inky depths, thanks to the Mystic Aquarium's Challenge of the Deep, which is part of Dr. Robert Ballard's Institute for Exploration (860–572–5955, www.mysticaquarium.org).

Ballard, who founded the institute and has a legacy of discoveries, including finding such sunken ships as the *Titanic* and *Bismarck,* conceived this wild, unusual multimedia experience. Challenge of the Deep, a simulated journey into the depths, starts with a seven-minute video in a spherical theater that takes you on your first 3,000-foot dive.

You won't blow your lunch aboard this ship.

Afterward, you are released into an interactive exhibit area that lets you poke around the world of artifacts and remote-sensing technology. There's fascinating stuff everywhere you look, but our favorite was the pressure sphere, where you climb down into a simulated submersible interior and get a feel for what a cramped, intimate vehicle it really is. Unlike the real deal, though, if you start feeling claustrophobic you just climb up a short ladder and you're safely back on "dry land." All in all, a most unusual and excellent adventure. See for yourself at Mystic Aquarium (55 Coogan Boulevard).

The Historical Worm Turns

Mystic

What do you do with a statue no one wants? You can move it around, but the vandals will still find it. Witness the sorry history of the statue of English officer John Mason, a controversial figure whose likeness just can't catch a break. The 110-year-old statue started its life on a twenty-three-ton granite block in Mystic, but in the early 1990s discussions began about having it moved. Meetings of an advisory committee about the statue sometimes devolved into shouting matches. There was no way to find compromise on Mason and his role in Connecticut and Native American history.

Eventually the bronze likeness was moved to Windsor after Native Americans in the Mystic area protested. It seems that Captain John Mason, the person, led the 1637 attack that nearly wiped out the Pequot tribe (the same tribe that now runs one of the hemisphere's most profitable casinos, just up the road in Ledyard).

The statue was moved to Windsor's Palisado Green, where it is periodically defaced. Once it was painted red, and the cleaning bill ran $1,500.

We Give You . . . Flagzilla!

New London

There, up ahead, flying in the breeze, is Flagzilla!

Well, "flying" is probably an overstatement. When you're this big, you more or less "float." And sometimes, you "tangle."

The Coast Guard Academy has impressive public displays through the year, but few are more eye-catching than the sight of their giant flag—affectionately known as "Flagzilla"—floating off the bow of the USCG *Barque Eagle*, the academy's floating classroom.

The ship is impressive even without the flag. The *Eagle*, a favorite, is 295 feet long, has a 4,400–pound anchor on the starboard (right) side, and couples that with a 3,500–pound anchor on the port. It hauls 140 cadets, but has room for 239. To keep the ship moving under sail, cadets are responsible for more than 22,300 square feet of sail and six miles of rigging.

Long may she wave . . . and flap . . . and scare seagulls.

It is no small feat to keep the ship afloat. Ironically, it was built in the '30s in Germany and used to train German Nazi sailors.

Today, the *Eagle* is the country's largest tall ship to fly the Stars and Stripes—which brings us back to Flagzilla, 30 by 60 feet of cloth, flown during special, in-port occasions. The flag is impressive in size—and depressing to keep untangled from the yardarm, or horizontal timbers of spars mounted on the ship's masts. So it's a very special occasion that will get Flagzilla out in public, and rare indeed that it will be flown at half-mast, where the opportunities for tangling are even greater.

For more information on the *Eagle*, visit www.cga.edu.

A Nice Place to Catch a Breeze
New London

Nathaniel Shaw was a sea captain who wanted a home on the Connecticut River. His granite mansion, built in the 1750s, once sat on the river's shore in New London—before dredging and development extended the shore away from his front door. During the Revolutionary War, the home was the state's naval office, and during the 1781 raid led by Benedict Arnold the mansion was supposed to have been destroyed but only the kitchen was damaged, and the structure remains.

The home is filled with history, but let's go to its backyard. Because New London summers could be so insufferably hot, the family also built a summer house on a hill behind their home. The small, octagonal structure is perfect for catching breezes from just about any direction. With the shutters closed and the windows open, said Edward Baker, executive director of the New London Historical Society, there's hardly a cooler place to be. And, as an added feature, the structure's domed ceiling makes it a "whisper room." Visitors can sit in any part of the small house, whisper, and be heard perfectly.

The summer house was probably built somewhere between 1785 and 1790. The society has photographs of Jane Richards Perkins, who sold her home to the society, serving tea there in the late nineteenth century.

The museum is open from 1:00 to 4:00 P.M. Sunday and Wednesday through Friday, and from 10:00 A.M. to 4:00 P.M. Saturday. For more information, call (860) 443–1209, or visit the Web site at www.newlondon history.org.

It's small, but oh so cool.

The Russians Are Here!

Niantic

We here in Nutmegland love our cultural diversity. Truly. If you wander around the state the way we have done, you can't help but stumble upon something cool from a foreign land that has put down some roots and bloomed. Obviously the most common manifestation of this (most welcome) international invasion is cuisine, for we do have our share of exotic restaurants that keep things fresh for those who like variety in their dining experience.

But on a sortie down Main Street in Niantic we made a really neat discovery: the Russians have truly invaded this cool coastal town, and in a very surprising way. In the past, we were afraid when the Russians would come it might be by submarine and we would be in peril (or at least in panic, if you've ever seen the hilarious film *The Russians Are Coming, The Russians Are Coming*).

This time, the Russians have infiltrated our state not with food or literature but with art, with the help of Dylan Gaffney. With the fall of the Soviet Union and the introduction of democracy in a land that had seen free expression stifled, Dylan was involved with an economic cooperation project in which Russian business types traveled here to promote investment opportunities. During this powwow Dylan encountered some genuine Russian arts and crafts, and got curious as to why there wasn't more promotion of this aspect of Russian culture. This experience inspired her to visit the country to see what she could see. She was absolutely blown away by the incredible passion of the Russian people in their artistic expression, and it moved her to want to help them introduce their works to a new audience in America. The result? Russia On the Sound at 396 Main Street (860–739–0067, www .russiaonthesound.org).

Nothing pleases us more than a peaceful invasion, especially one that involves art. And what type of works from a faraway culture are waiting for you at this facility? Take a good look at Olga Topanina's amazing sign outside the gallery. It's really quite striking, and the unique and warm nature of her work is a brilliant intro into the special appeal of the Russian experience. Curious? Sojourn down to Niantic and have a look at how former "enemies" become neighbors.

From King Tut to Bogey

Niantic

When you start probing the contents of an antiques store, it's not unusual to see some strange stuff—but it is unusual to have one of the artifacts actually stare back at you.

What's even weirder is when the antique doing the staring is a dead ringer for Rick in *Casablanca,* and he seems to want to tell you that he sticks his neck out for nobody.

But such an encounter is typical at the Thames Trading Company at 55 Main Street in Niantic (860–691–1272). This is a very unusual place, with some really rare birds lurking both indoors and out, including a King Tut sarcophagus, miniature Eiffel Tower, and an entire division of lawn Buddhas.

"The collection is really kind of tame at the moment, believe it or not," observes owner Steve Femiak. "We've had some really weird and great things here, like a full-size Louis Armstrong, a Babe Ruth, more than twenty giraffes, and things like that. We started out with gargoyles because one time I had about 700 shipped in from England. The stuff comes from all over the world, including local auctions."

The international flavor of the store is one of the things that makes it so special, and it's not surprising when you realize that Steve has spent a lot of time and money bringing things to Connecticut from all over the globe.

"I went crazy one year and brought in twenty-two containers of items; we had hundreds of cast-iron urns; hundreds of statues, including dogs and huge lions; and all kinds of stuff," Steve recounts. "I feel like the place is tame right now compared with what we had at our old location, which we moved from not long ago after being there for fifteen years. But we're getting the inventory, and we'll be back at those levels soon."

We may have discovered where garden gnomes and their ilk go when they hold a convention.

By the Sea, By the Sea
Niantic

People who walk Niantic's shore have 1,000 or more reasons to stop, and counting

When fifty benches were offered to people to buy memorial plaques along the newly renovated Niantic Bay Overlook, the benches were snatched up immediately. So the town began to think bigger. A fence by the mile-and-a-tenth boardwalk would make a lovely place for small, $100 plaques, wouldn't it? A town in Massachusetts had offered a similar way to memorialize loved ones, and had done well. So the town's official Plaque Committee (really just two men, Bill Rinoski and Andy Pappas) began accepting sentiments to go on small plaques to be affixed to the long fence.

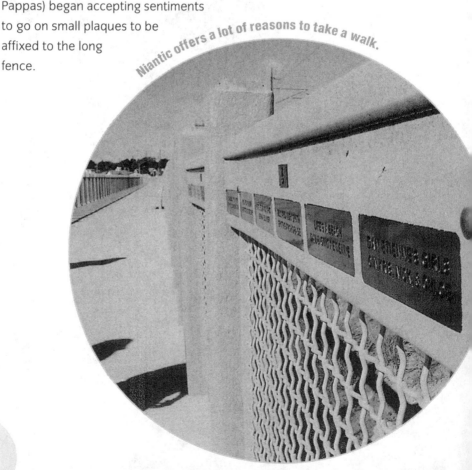

Niantic offers a lot of reasons to take a walk.

The men had no idea what they would start. Requests came in from twenty states and around the world. It seems just about everyone has a connection to the sea in Niantic. Some of the messages are straightforward: BOB, SEE YOU WHEN MY CHORES ARE DONE. Some leave Rinoski and Pappas wondering. ALICE—HER SMILE WAS HER LV. LV? Love? Live? Roman numerals for fifty-five? Such mysteries turn a walk along the fence into a much longer commitment than you'd imagine. What does it all mean?

So far, the men have refused only messages that include phone numbers. That one rule keeps out the riffraff, and cuts down on the commercial messages. Nearly every day, the committee sits back and marvels at the need for people to memorialize their loved ones by the sea.

For more information on the Niantic Bay Overlook, visit www.nianticboardwalk.org.

The Disneyland of Bookstores
Niantic

You've got to love it when you pull into a parking lot and you're greeted by a big, shaggy, friendly dog. When was the last time that happened to you at a major book chain, hmmm? Most of the bookstores in the malls have no such welcoming parties; in fact, you are often confronted by massive security guards who have no desire to discuss serious literature.

The Book Barn at 41 West Main Street in Niantic (860 739 5715, www.bookbarnniantic.com) is not just different from such cold, impersonal places. It's a different world altogether, which you realize not only after the canine greets you but also as you walk toward the barn itself and see that it's not just a bookstore (for used and rare, out-of-print books) but more of a book village. In satellite buildings arranged in a little town outside, there's even a pen with sheep and goats and small sheds where different types of used books are bought and sold.

"We're unique, and part of this was driven simply by the geography," explains owner Randi White. "When we started here in the basement of the barn in 1988, we just rented the room where we sold books. We kept renting more and more of the barn and then other buildings on the property; it seemed that we'd expand every four years or so, and we almost put ourselves out of business! But it's always worked out in the end, and now we own the buildings. Our business continues to grow, and now I've got twelve employees."

The barn itself is cozy (and well stocked with all manner of literature and the odd content feline), and the employees Randi mentioned are as enthusiastic and devoted to the book trade as he is. All in all it's an unusually cool place to roam around—and you don't even have to be looking for a book.

You may come for the literature, but you'll stay for the atmosphere.

The Birds Have Nothing on Abbott's in the Rough

Noank

When Alfred Hitchcock was filming *The Birds* in 1961 at Bodega Bay, he had no idea he was accurately reflecting life for diners at Abbott's Lobsters in the Rough.

Well, almost. The seagulls at this, one of Connecticut's best and best-loved lobster shacks, are downright cheeky, even though they don't actually attack humans. The restaurant does what it can, like stretch taut wires over the dining area, but the birds have been known to carry off the stray lobster tail, the wayward potato chip, even plastic cutlery—although what they would need that for is beyond us.

Other rumors say they've carried off a camera, a small child, and an equally small watercraft. We suspect those last three missing items are made up, though. Just know that seasoned diners at the seaside shack know enough to never, ever leave their food unattended for fear of losing it, all of it, to hungry gulls. If you can beat away the wildlife, the lobster is utterly delicious, and Abbott's offers outdoor dining with a view of the ship traffic up and down the Mystic River channel.

Plus—we recommend the carrot cake—the desserts are great.

You can't see them here, but just off-camera the seagulls are plotting.

Abbott's even offers a do-it-yourself lobster bake, all in its own canister. Each canister comes with a lobster, a sweet potato, an ear of corn, steamers, mussels, and a white potato, all packed in fresh seaweed. Simply heat on the stove, and eat up! Abbott's also delivers.

The seasonal restaurant is at 117 Pearl Street in Noank, just south of Mystic. Call (860) 536–7719 for hours, or visit www.abbotts-lobster .com.

A Cast of Thousands
Norwich

John Slater was the Bill Gates of his time. He operated mills in Jewett City and Hopeville, Connecticut, and he directed many other companies, including the Norwich and New London Steamboat Company. In 1882 he donated $1 million for the education of southern "Freed Men." In 1884, the year of Slater's death, his son William decided to donate a museum in his honor to the Norwich Free Academy.

A principal there at the time, Dr. Robert Porter Keep, was a Greek author of some renown. He suggested that the museum house Greek casts—

Athena awaits you.

plaster replicas of all the biggies from the Greek pantheon and else-where. The effect is room after room of eerie-white statutes that look as though they've walked off a movie set.

The Slater cast collection is still one of the largest in the country. The museum was built by the CCC during the Depression and has an impressive slate roof and many marble columns. The Slater Museum, which is part of the Norwich Free Academy campus, is at 108 Crescent Avenue (Route 2) in Norwich; exit 81E off I–395. For hours call (860) 887–2506.

Up, Up, and Away
Norwich

Fancy making a huge statement about your love of America? Fancy making a statement that's along the lines of the head of the Statue of Liberty, 105 feet high, soaring over the heads of some really jealous earth-dwellers?

Eastern Connecticut Balloon Services, Inc., has the balloon for you. Brothers (and veteran balloonists) Gerard and Mark Lefevre have designed and manufactured the Liberty Head hot air balloon in a shape that's three and a half times larger than the real Lady Liberty's head in New York Harbor. They also have a full-scale replica of the Statue of Lib-erty, named Free Lady, made in 1986, the real statue's centennial. She's an FAA registered aircraft and stands 170 feet tall.

If that doesn't get the attention of the ground-dwellers, the Lefevres also have The Hammer, a 120-foot-tall, well, hammer. They also offer rides in more conventional balloons—with reservations, of course. Bal-looning season in eastern Connecticut runs from April through Decem-ber, but Eastern will fly any time, weather permitting. For more info, call (860) 376–5807, or visit the Web site at www.easternctballoon.com.

GEORGE WASHINGTON ATE HERE. NO, REALLY.

Thomas Leffingwell may have begun building the Leffingwell Inn in 1675. His grandson, Christopher Leffingwell, inherited the house in 1756. Leffingwell, who expanded the original two-room house to include three parlors, ran a knitting factory, a stoneware factory, a paper factory, a chocolate factory, and several trading ships. He was also justice of the peace, and held court in the dining room. Court papers were stored behind wall panels, as these were precloset days.

Leffingwell often opened his home to Washington's troops and was supposed to have dined with him, but Washington had to decline because he was busy with 10,000 troops.

The Leffingwell Inn, now a museum, is at 348 Washington Street in Norwich. From Hartford, go to the end of Route 2 and take a left at the stoplight. The first left is the driveway to the museum. Or call (860) 889–9440 for information.

SOUTHEAST

Pray for Us Gamblers, Now and at the Time of Our Losses, Amen
Norwich

For years, Norwich resident Salvatore Verdirome maintained a bevy of bathtub Madonnas in his three-acre backyard that rather quickly became a shrine to area gamblers. The carpenter said he'd had a vision that included the Virgin Mary—who said something he didn't quite catch—and so he turned his steep yard into a terraced garden of statues of the saints, the Virgin Mary, and Jesus.

His faith didn't stop with sculpture. Verdirome also collected day-old doughnuts to give to the city's poor. He gathered bottles and cans and donated the money for food for the homeless. Despite the town's general discomfort with his project, gamblers at the nearby casinos came to appreciate the shrines—known as the Sanctuary of Love—as a nice place to pray for providence before dropping their cash, and a good place to come to pray for forgiveness afterward. Over time, Verdirome added other religious scenes, including Stations of the Cross and the Ten Commandments. He charged no admission, but relied on supplicants for donations.

Alas, Mr. Verdirome became ill in 2000, and was placed in a nursing home. The city auctioned off the statues two years later. He died in 2004.

The Fastest Garage in the World
Old Lyme

You have to watch those brash young men. Quite often what starts as a dream (that seems unattainable) will make way, in time, for a stunning success in a related field.

Additionally, when it comes to Connecticut, you never know what kind of world-famous concern might be hiding in the woods, quietly going about the business of world-class engineering where you would least expect it.

Given this information, it should come as no surprise that as a brash young man growing up in Darien (OK, he was probably not brash at all—just determined), Reeves Callaway dreamed of being a professional race car driver. Incidentally, while he was dreaming, his father left his job at Burlington Northern and started Callaway wines in California and later Callaway golf clubs, both of which were (and are) wildly successful businesses.

Meanwhile, young Reeves acquired a fine education at Amherst and pursued his dream of becoming a professional racer. He actually did quite well, but even after winning an SCCA National Championship in 1973 couldn't get the financial backing to continue his career. However, his considerable racing experience both as driver and engineer led him to open a garage behind his house in Old Lyme. Thus, in 1976, Callaway Cars (860–434–9002, www.callawaycars.com) was born.

"I never really expected it to become a big deal," reflects Callaway, who these days lives mostly in California while the company thrives in Old Lyme. "We initially called it Mediocre Motors among ourselves. We were literally just fixing cars and making turbocharger conversions for BMWs, Volkswagens, and other high-quality European cars. This was a traditional, back-of-the-house operation; we had five or six people work-ing, cars all over the lawn, the septic tank bubbling out of the ground, and a refrigerator too small to hold everybody's lunch."

But boy oh boy, did this place get a great reputation. Callaway and his crew were doing amazing things with engine and chassis develop-ment and got noticed by some very big names. Ultimately, something amazing happened in 1985.

"Chevrolet called us," explains Callaway, "and asked, 'Would you consider turbocharging some Corvettes for us?' Well, we responded with the question, 'Does Dolly Parton sleep on her back?' Of course we'd consider it!"

The 200+ mph Callaway Corvette is just one of the company's many triumphs, and Callaway Cars now designs production engines for the likes of Aston Martin, Land Rover, Holden, and others in addition to General Motors. The cars just keep getting faster, and among auto aficionados Old Lyme is now as famous as Detroit, thanks to a little operation at 3 High Street.

"For a little thirty-man company in Connecticut, I'm really happy with the reputation we have escaped with," laughs Callaway.

You can have your twin turbos tuned here.

Most Times She Feels like a Nut

Old Lyme

For nearly forty years, Elizabeth Tashjian has been extolling the virtues of nuts—peanuts, pine nuts, and what she says is the world's largest nut, a thirty-five-pound coco-de-mer grown on an island in the Indian Ocean. The entire first floor of her Victorian mansion was devoted to her personal nut museum. She opened the museum on a whim, and since then, with missionary zeal she's matched wits with the likes of Johnny Carson, David Letterman, and Howard Stern. At her 1981 debut on the Carson show, Johnny loved her so much that he brought her back a month later. The second time she was on for twenty minutes, a lifetime on Carson. The museum contained nut sculptures (Tashjian is an artist), nut masks, and a general nutty decor.

"Those who come are prepared for something different," Elizabeth says. "It requires courage to cross the threshold."

Ill health forced Elizabeth from her museum, but her work lives on in a traveling art exhibit, courtesy of Connecticut College.

The Warmth in the Corner

Old Saybrook

There is a fine line between loony and innovative. Also, there are a lot of famous architects out there, and it's safe to say that many of the icons of the art have graced future generations with innovations that may have seemed goofy at first glance. Yet these same ideas have made modern living much more enjoyable.

At the same time, a lot of really clever architectural ideas have come from simple folks who, in the process of constructing a safe, cozy home for their families, have come up with some wonderfully weird or elegant (depending on your point of view) designs.

The William Hart House at 350 Main Street in Old Saybrook (860–388–2622, www.oldsaybrook.com) has a really novel design in terms of home heating that at first must have seemed pretty weird. The conventional wisdom of the time (around 1767) had fireplaces in the center of the room in order to spread their warmth and make it easy to toast marshmallows—which is wild because they hadn't been invented yet.

But Hart placed the fireplaces in the corners, with four units for four rooms exiting into a common chimney on each side of the house, respectively. Very clever, and very space efficient—it really looks kind of neat, too. This design was rare at the time and was probably regarded as odd, but there are other examples from the period around New England.

A house with warm corners.

A Singular Sundae
Old Saybrook

In New York City it's not unusual for a famous individual to get a sandwich dedicated in his or her honor, especially if the celebrity in question is a regular patron of a well-known delicatessen. But here in Connecticut we've done the Big Apple one better by dedicating an ice-cream sundae to a rather special individual—a charming lady who presided over one of the most famous pharmacies in New England.

Miss Anna Louise James was the first African-American pharmacist in the state. Miss James ran the James Pharmacy at the corner of Pennywise Lane for half a century, from 1917 until 1967.

Where tasteful treats honor the past.

Incidentally, one regular patron of the general store associated with the pharmacy during that time may be familiar to you: Katharine Hepburn.

A major fixture of this Old Saybrook landmark (860–395–1229, www.pratthouse.net/jamesgallery.htm) is the soda fountain, which has most of the original furnishings dating back to the '40s (including the milkshake machine). A specialty of the house is the Miss James Dusty Road Sundae (a sprinkle of malt powder accounts for the name), which has been enjoyed by patrons for many years—tasteful tribute to a dedicated pharmacist. Her former place of business is still a soda fountain, but the pharmacy is now also an art gallery, and the upstairs is a bed-and-breakfast called the Pratt House.

The building itself was originally the general store for the Humphrey Pratt Tavern, and it is said that even Lafayette was a customer.

"He either purchased a bar of saddlesoap or a pair of socks," muses the James Gallery and Soda Fountain's Diane Aiknoras. "We're really not sure, because these stories tend to get kind of screwed up over time."

America's Oldest Government Lighthouse
Stonington

In 1823 ships at sea were warned away from Stonington's rocky coast by a large light atop a 30-foot tower. The light was actually ten oil lamps and parabolic reflectors to increase their brightness. But sea and wind beat the tower, and in 1840 it was dismantled and reassembled at what is now 7 Water Street in Stonington Borough, with a larger structure that included living quarters for the lighthouse keeper. The light stayed active until 1889, when a new light was built on an equally new break-water built to protect Stonington Harbor.

The Stonington Historical Society opened the Old Lighthouse Museum in the old lighthouse in 1925; today the museum houses everything Stonington, including an impressive collection of Stonington stoneware made in or around the village between 1780 and 1834.

Visitors who climb up the stone steps to the tower can get a view of three states, if you count Connecticut. Call ahead at (860) 535–1440, or visit the Web site at www .stoningtonhistory.org.

This beacon still beckons.

Now I Lay Me in the Deep

Stonington

The sea has always been a widow maker among the fishing families of the village of Stonington, which may contribute to fishers' reputation of being a superstitious lot. Superstitious, and religious, and so even though precious few fishing vessels remain in the port, the fleet has for nearly fifty years had an official blessing to remember the dead, and forestall anyone joining them in Davy Jones' locker.

Stonington houses the last surviving fishing fleet in the state, and the Portuguese influence is still strong. The Blessing of the Fleet started in 1954 as a celebration and a memorial. It includes a parade through town, and on the sea, a blessing by a regional Catholic bishop as boats pass by in watery procession, and then a memorial wreath with a symbolic broken anchor is thrown into the sea.

The Blessing of the Fleet is usually held toward the end of July or early August each year.

As Sands in the Hour Glass, So Is the Movement of This Island

Stonington

Nothing is forever, including a tiny slip of sand in Little Narragansett Bay called Sandy Point. Although most of it remains in Rhode Island, it wants very much to be in Connecticut. For centuries the land, buffeted by wind and tide, has been moving toward the Connecticut shore.

Sandy Point was once a part of Napatree Point, just off Watch Hill, Rhode Island. A devastating hurricane in 1938 split the tip and turned Sandy Point into an island. Not long afterwards, an Alfred Gildersleeve bought the land and used it for duck hunting and swimming. But it isn't just the ducks that find the island inviting. Sandy Point is also a popular landing spot for hawks, peregrine falcons, American oystercatchers, and roseate terns.

As boating became more popular in the '50s and '60s, Gildersleeve opened half the land for public use. His family eventually deeded the land to what was once the Mashantucket Land Trust, now the Avalonia Land Convervancy.

Meanwhile, in '97, the point split again into two islands.

Now, the land is moving northwest at roughly 2½ yards a year. Members of the conservancy say it's only a matter of time before it finally bumps against the Connecticut coast.

Star Light, Star Bright—Place Your Bets
Uncasville

If you're a dedicated stargazer, you're always excited when there's a new tool available to study the stars. The Hubble telescope (once they fixed it) is a great example of a breakthrough device that has greatly enhanced our view of the heavens and it has helped increase our knowledge of our celestial neighbors.

Wouldn't it be cool to have one of those puppies hovering over your house, beaming down the latest goings on around Betelgeuse onto your big-screen TV?

Well, Connecticut may not have our own personal hovering Hubbles, but we do have the world's largest planetarium dome. And where is this marvel, you ask? UConn? Yale? On the property of some private contractor like United Technologies, who built the suits our astronauts wore on the moon?

WHAT UNCAS NEEDED WAS A GOOD PRESS AGENT

When James Fenimore Cooper wrote *The Last of the Mohicans*, people confused it with the Mohegans, a tribe in southeast Connecticut that was thought to have been all but decimated by a surprise attack by the neighboring Pequots, who were aiding the Europeans in the mid-1600s.

(That same tribe is now the proud sponsor of one of the world's largest gambling establishments, second only, perhaps, to that of their neighbors—the Mashantucket Pequots.)

However, there really was an Uncas, as Mr. Cooper wrote, and he really did lead his people in times of trial, but there the similarity ends.

Meet the real Uncas—or, at least, see his grave—at the Indian Burial Grounds on Sachem Street, off Route 32, in Uncasville.

Of course not. This is Connecticut, and we stick such things in casinos, silly. Or at least the Mohegan Sun Casino in Uncasville (800–226–7711, www.mohegansun.com) does, in their new development called the Casino in the Sky.

The planetarium itself displays changing constellations, sun cycles, clouds, and even the aurora borealis (or northern lights, which are really cool). If you think having such a heavenly display in a casino is weird, wilder yet is what's immediately beneath the dome—a huge structure called Wombi Rock.

Reminiscent of the Fortress of Solitude in the first *Superman* movie, the rock is a three-story crystal mountain built of more than 12,000 individual plates of onyx and alabaster fused to glass.

There is a bar at the top just under the dome, so you can sip martinis while you search the universe for intelligent life. If you feel the need to do some wagering, the games are just a short stroll away.

iNDEX

INDEX

INDEX

INDEX

INDEX

About the Authors

Born in Kentucky, Susan Campbell grew up mostly in the Ozarks of Missouri. She moved to Connecticut for what she assumed would be a brief assignment, during which she intended to observe up close the Yankee subculture (Yankee of the "Doodle Dandy" variety, not Yankees–George Steinbrenner variety, although they're an interesting group as well). That was 1986. Since then, her biggest fear is that she's losing her Ozark accent. Susan is an award-winning columnist at the *Hartford Courant* and lives in Marlborough with her husband and their two sons.

A Connecticut resident by way of Texas, Los Angeles, and New York, Bill Heald went on hiatus from the motion picture industry in 1993 and started freelance writing. A frequent contributor to several motorcycle publications and Web sites, he also has penned articles for *Stuff, The Robb Report,* and *Northeast* magazine. He also regularly reviews automobiles for Remindernet Publications, and motorcycles for *Penthouse* and *Backroads* magazines. Bill has written about everything from horse racing to lawn tractors, and currently lives in Hampton with a woman he doesn't deserve and several four-legged companions.

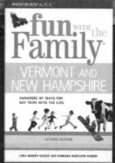
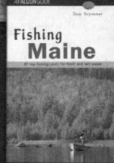